DR W GRAHAM
SCROGGIE
ON
Matthew & Mark

ARK PUBLISHING
130 City Road, London EC1V 2NJ

CHRISTIAN LITERATURE CRUSADE
Fort Washington, Pennsylvania 19034

Also in this series:
Scroggie on Luke and John
Scroggie on Acts and 1 & 2 Corinthians
Scroggie on Galatians to Jude
Scroggie on The Psalms

©1981 **Ark Publishing** (UK dist.)
130 City Road, London EC1V 2NJ

Christian Literature Crusade (USA dist.)
Box C, Ft. Washington, PA 19034

First published 1981

ISBN 0 86201 091 8 (UK)
ISBN 0 87508 484 2 (USA)

Printed in U.S.A.

Foreword

Dr. Graham Scroggie's works need no introduction. As an outstanding expositor of God's Word and a greatly loved pastor he became widely known, not only in the United Kingdom and the United States of America, but far beyond. His periods as minister of Charlotte Chapel, Edinburgh (1916-1933), and Spurgeon's Metropolitan Tabernacle, London (1938-1944), testify to his powers of preaching and exposition, as week by week he fed crowded congregations with the Word of God.

Dr. Scroggie's gifts found further expression through his participation in Scripture Union's worldwide Bible reading programme. From 1927 to 1931 he was a regular contributor to Daily Notes, a series of expository and devotional readings which brought him into daily contact with hundreds of thousands of readers. Those notes are now made available in book form for the first time, not only for those who remember this great Bible teacher, but for all those who will value his clear insight into the enduring lessons of God's Word made personally applicable through the twin gifts of his incisive mind and warm devotion to Christ. Dr. Scroggie's selections are designed to be read together with the Scriptures themselves, to which he regularly turns the reader. His Bible was primarily the King James Version, and his use of this particular text has been consistently retained in the five volumes now published.

Today's reader may wish to follow Scroggie through the Scriptures on a daily basis — each page contains a reading complete in itself — and this was Scroggie's original intention. However, the readings are so designed that one may also move uninterruptedly through each volume without break. They are written as a valuable study and devotional aid and therefore stand in their own right as Bible commentaries to which the reader may turn again and again.

Matthew's Gospel

Contents

Matthew's Gospel

Matthew was a Greek-speaking Jewish Christian setting out to demonstrate how Christianity is the fulfilment of God's saving purpose for his people begun in the Old Testament dispensation. A simple. rhyme expresses it like this:

'Matthew gives us five discourses;
In threes and sevens he likes his sources,
He writes to show what the O.T. meant,
With an ecclesiastic bent.'

The tidy mind of the custom clerk (9:9) is seen in the arrangement of his material. The five great discourses, each ending with words like 'When Jesus had ended these sayings' (7:28) are: the Sermon on the Mount (5-7); the Charge to the Twelve (10); the Parables of the Kingdom (13); True Greatness and Forgiveness (18); and the Parables of the End (24,25).

Jesus, who came not to abolish, but to fulfil the law and the prophets (5:17), is hailed as 'Son of David' no less than eight times. He is the man born to be King, the Lawgiver of the new *ecclesia* (church) of the true people of God. Alone among the evangelists Matthew uses the word 'church' (16:18; 18:17).

Alongside the distinctively Jewish features, we must not, however, overlook his universalism. The field is the world (13:38); Gentile 'wise men' come at the beginning to worship the infant Messiah (2:1-12); at the close the great commission is to 'teach all nations' (28:19). His Gospel begins with 'Emmanuel . . . God with us' (1:23) and concludes, 'Lo, I am with you alway' (28:20).

Matthew probably wrote his Gospel quite soon after the destruction of the Temple and the city of Jerusalem.

Jesus

This is a passage of personalities: we shall concentrate on the seven mentioned in verses 18 to 25.

1. **Mary.** From what is recorded we see her to be a simple, humble, chaste, gifted and devout young woman of Davidic descent. Look up in the Gospel records all that is said of her.

2. **Joseph.** We see him to be 'a righteous man', God-fearing, courageous, and devoted to Mary his espoused. The situation brought to him both pain and a problem and he turned aside to think it out in the presence of the Lord. Is that what you do with your problems and pains?

3. **An Angel.** Luke tells us it was Gabriel. Look up all that the Bible tells us of this 'man-of-God'.

4. **A Prophet.** We know this was Isaiah. Look up the passage, Isaiah 7:14, and mark the context. You will observe that the giving of the name *Emmanuel* to our Lord was the *final* but not the *first* fulfilment of this prophecy.

5. **The Holy Spirit.** Follow out the place and power of the Spirit in the life and work of Jesus, beginning at this point. At every stage the Holy Spirit is in evidence, showing that the whole manifestation was divine.

6. **People** (21). These are referred to, to remind us of our fallen state and our need of a Saviour. *Sins* supplies us with the reason for this event.

7. **Jesus.** He is central in the story. Mark these three truths among others: ● *His miraculous birth.* Jesus had no human father. The Virgin birth is not open to challenge: it is fact, and was a necessity. ● *His mysterious person.* That he was born of a woman shows that he is *human*: that he was conceived in her of the Holy Spirit shows that he is *divine*. He was and is both God and Man. ● *His merciful work.* 'He shall save from sins' (21); you from yours, me from mine.

Thought: Joyful news—Jesus saves.

A new factor enters into human history

This is pre-eminently **the gospel of the King: his person,** 1:1 to 4:11; **his purpose,** 4:12 to 16:12; and **his passion,** 16:13 to 28:20.

Under **the person of the King** (1:1-4:11), we have *his ancestry,* 1:1-17; *his advent,* 1:18 to 2:23; *his ambassador,* 3:1-12; and *his advance,* 3:13 to 4:11. That is our outline for the next four readings.

His ancestry is traced from Abraham to David (1:1-6), David to Zedekiah (1:6-11) and Zedekiah to Jesus (1:11-17).

The record of **his advent** calls attention to three things: *his divine origin* 1:18-23; *his human birth* 1:24,25, and *his early infancy*—in Bethlehem 2:1-12; in Egypt 2:13-18; and in Nazareth 2:19-23. Put this outline in your Bible margin. The passages which precede Matthew's record are, Luke 1:1-4; John 1:1-18; Luke 1:5-80.

The first impressive fact in this reading is that the Creator and Sovereign of all things became a helpless babe. Thereby he has for ever sanctified both motherhood and babyhood. His infancy, as all infancy, was characterised by impotence, innocence and ignorance. Little did he know what influences were circling around and playing upon him; the love of his mother, the wonder of the Magi, the hate of Herod, and the worship of the angels (Hebrews 1:6). Observe also that the Saviour of the world drew to himself from his birth the attention of both Jews and Gentiles, and, significantly enough, it was the Gentiles who received him (2). When this babe arrived Philosophy knelt (11), but Government clenched its fist (13). On a certain spot, and in a certain hour God entered into human history by adding our humanity to his deity. Infinite mystery, and eternal mercy!

Thought: Christ will be found of all who seek him.

By way of Egypt to Nazareth

Jesus, who was born in *Bethlehem* (1), is now taken into *Egypt* (13), and later, to *Nazareth* (23). Look up these places on the map, or better, draw a map outline, and mark in these places. The only time that Jesus was out of Palestine was when, as an infant, he was taken to Egypt, where he remained about two years.

Why did Joseph, Mary and the babe leave Bethlehem (13)? At what time was the journey undertaken (14)? Until what event did they remain there (15)? What Old Testament passage was then fulfilled (15)? What resulted from this flight (16)? Where does this result connect with the Old Testament (17,18)? Jesus was born about 6 B.C.: Herod died in 4 B.C.

That God protected the infant son of Mary is not to be wondered at: that he should have allowed this slaughter of the innocents must ever remain a mystery. Do not suppose that what is predicted is necessarily ordained of God. What he does not decree he foresees, and in this case he forewarned (13).

Mark the activities of *angels*, the employment of *dreams*, and the fulfilment of *prophecies* in connection with Jesus' infancy. No definite passage can be found for verse 23. Isaiah, Jeremiah and Zechariah had all referred to the Messiah as the *Branch*, in Hebrew, *'Nezer'*, and this suggested *Nazarene*.

For thirty years Jesus was to live at Nazareth, a place physically beautiful, but morally corrupt (John 1:46), commanding the scenes of many of the most stirring events of Israel's history, and on the highway along which traders, travellers, and Roman legions passed to and fro. This child had a simple and pious home and upbringing. Luke tells the story (2:40-52).

Thought: Let us trust God for unconscious protection.

King and ambassador meet

In thinking of the **the King's ambassador** (3:1-12) we should consider *the man*, (1-4), *the mission* (5,6), and *the message* (7-12). John the Baptist was about 18 months older than Jesus, and occupied a unique place among the Old Testament prophets in that he was the last of that order. He was built on severe and ascetic lines, and belongs to the fellowship of such as Elijah, Cromwell, and John Knox. Perhaps many of his day did not like his 'style', but that was because it had teeth as well as a tongue, a sting as well as a hiss.

His utterances were not in polished periods but in undecorated terms. His words fell upon religious hypocrites as the battle-axes of our Saxon forefathers upon the helmets of their foes. We need men like him today. There is so much oily talk, and velvety touch whereby nobody is hurt because nobody is hit. Oh, for a man in high places who would talk to the common-sense and conscience of the people, who, with the besom of passionate sincerity, would sweep out the Augean stables; who would tell proud, corrupt people the truth about themselves, who would stand uncompromisingly for living principles, and who, in his own life, would exemplify them. Such was this John.

And now we come to **the King's advance**, (3:13-4:11) and three things claim our attention: *his condescension* (13-15), *his consecration* (16,17), and *his conflict* (4:1-11). Jesus' baptism was an act of identification with his nation, and is quite distinct from Christian baptism. Here is the second recorded utterance of Jesus (15). The first is in Luke 2:49. The path is ever the path of blessing; the loyal heart shall see the opened heavens. Christ calls us to go with him all the way.

Thought: The Spirit is alike the cause and the effect of spirituality.

Deadly antagonists

The subject here is *the conflict of the King*, and with it ends the first main division of this Gospel. Study this story by answering the questions, Who? When? Where? What? How? Why?

Remember, no human being was with Jesus in this ordeal, so that we are entirely dependent upon him for the particulars of it. To challenge any part of this story is to challenge the veracity of Christ. We are not told whether the temptation was objective or subjective. In any case, what matters is the reality of it. We must believe that this, which is the supreme temptation of many (Luke 22:28), is both fundamental and comprehensive. For this reason Milton chose it for his *Paradise Regained*. Almost certainly it is referred to in the passage, he *'was in all points tempted like as we are, yet without sin'* (Hebrews 4:15).

There are three levels on which each of us can be tempted: the lowest is the *body*, the highest is the *spirit*, and the central is the *soul*, and a different appeal is made to each. Jesus was tempted on each of these levels: the body—*feed yourself*; the spirit—*cast yourself down from a height and let God's angels take care of you*; the soul—*worship me, and I'll give you all the kingdoms of the world*.

The first bait was *selfishness*, the second was *presumption*, and the third was *compromise*. Think about that, and say by which of these you are most tempted, and whether or not you fall. Jesus won on each level, and with *'the sword of the Spirit, which is the word of God'*. These are the cardinal temptations, *'the desire of the flesh'*, *'the pride of life'*, and *'the desire of the eyes'*. Eve fell to all of them in a *garden*. Christ conquered all of them in a *desert*. There is no need to live a defeated life.

Thought: A rusty sword means a ruined soul.

The beginning of Jesus' ministry

Here we enter upon the second main division of this Gospel—the purpose of the King (4:12 to 16:12), which let us divide into four parts: the enunciation of his principles (4:12 to 7:29); the demonstration of his authority (8:1 to 9:34); the promulgation of his message (9:35 to 11:30); and the opposition to his claims (12:1 to 16:12). Under the first of these falls our present reading: *The inception of the kingdom* (4:12-25), where consider, the place, the message, the agents, the result.

● **The place is Capernaum** (12-16). Why did Jesus leave Nazareth (Luke 4:17-30)? Capernaum, the modern *Tell Hum* is situated on the N.W. border of the Lake of Galilee. Matthew applies Isaiah 8:11 to 9:6, to Christ's settlement there. When John's work was arrested, Jesus began his (12). God's workers drop out, but his work goes on. Capernaum was Jesus' centre of work throughout his Galilean ministry. Every worker should have a base of operations. Don't be a religious tramp.

● **The message** (17). It conerns the *kingdom,* and it calls for *repentance* on the part of all who would be subjects: the two great notes are, *authority* and *submission.* The expression *kingdom of heaven* occurs in this Gospel only: find out how many times. The history of it is set forth parabolically in chapter 13.

● **The agents** (18-22). Christ needed and needs helpers. Now he chose four, two pairs of brothers, and all fishermen. In calling them the Master spiritualises nature (19): theirs will be the same task, only in another realm. Is your response to Christ's call *straightway* (20-22)? They are doubly blessed who obey at once.

● **The result** (23-25). *Teaching, preaching, healing* define the form of Jesus' ministry, and the words, *multitudes* and *miracles,* summarise his ministry.

Thought: Encouragement is an inspiration, not a foundation.

What counts in the world

Under **the enunciation of his principles** (4:12 to 7:29), the second section is *the manifesto of the King* (chapters 5 to 7); commonly called the Sermon on the Mount, wherein we are shown who are *the subjects of the kingdom*, what are *its fundamental truths*, and *the way of entrance into it*. Luke also records this sermon, but of Matthew's 107 verses, he gives only 30.

This particular portion tells of *the subjects of the kingdom* as to their *character* and *influence* (3-12, 13-16). These are, of course, vitally related, for one's influence can never be better than one's character. And we should learn this also, that the thing of primary importance is not influence, but character. What you are is always of more importance than what you do; and what you do derives its value from what you are: that is the broad lesson of our portion.

But look at it more closely. *Blessed* occurs nine times, and excepting verses 3 and 10 is related to the future — *shall*. Mark carefully what Jesus says about *lowliness, sorrow, submissiveness, earnest desire, mercifulness, purity, peaceableness* and *endurance*. Verse 11 is verse 10 applied to the disciples. All these qualities should characterise us, and we are *blessed* only as they do. Such a character as this will exercise a true and great influence, both without (13,14), and within (15,16).

Christian influence should be *preservative as salt*, and *illuminative as light*. Salt does not make what is bad better, but prevents it from getting worse. Light reveals and banishes the darkness. We may relate the *'city on a hill'* to the Christian in the world, and the *'candle in the house'* to the Christian in the church. As salt, have you lost your pungency? As light, have you lost your brightness? We are here to arrest the progress of evil, and to advance the kingdom of God. Are you doing it?

Thought: You be what others should become.

Right within

After *the subjects of the kingdom*, the Sermon presents *the word of the kingdom*, relative first to *law*, (17-48), and then to *life* (6:1 to 7:6).

First then, *the word of the kingdom* relative to *law*; the *letter* of it (17-20), and the *spirit* of it (21-48). Though Christ and Moses may well be contrasted, they are never opposed. Revelation does not contradict itself. The Old Covenant was as truly of God as is the New. The law was the forerunner of the gospel. Jesus came not to destroy what had gone before, but to *fulfil* it, and to *fill* it with a new content. Christ did not stand for legal righteousness (20). There was a way of keeping the law which was really a breaking of it.

And so Jesus calls attention from the *letter* to the *spirit* of the law in six particulars, relative to *murder* (21-26), *adultery* (27-30), *divorce* (31,32), *oaths* (33-37), *retaliation* (38-42), and *love* (43-48).

Relative to *murder* (21-26), Jesus teaches that we shall be judged not only by what we do but also by what we would do if we dare. The spirit of murder is far more widespread than the practice of it, for obvious reasons. The *anger* which is the spirit that would hurt another is incipient murder. By *raca* and *fool* is meant *blockhead*, and *blackguard*; the one denied the intellectual value of a man, and the other, his religious worth. No man can be religious who is immoral (23,24); no man can be right with God and wrong with his brother. The higher righteousness will lead a man to do all he can to put wrong right. This we should do, not for fear of consequences, but because it is our moral duty so to do.

Thought: Don't put the second duty before the first.

Sword thrusts

Read carefully and solemnly verses 27-32, which treat of **adultery and divorce**, for both these sins, in one form or another, are still very prevalent. Let not a false modesty prevent us facing the facts. Uncleanness is not confined to physical acts, it is to be found in mental attitudes. We are condemned, not only for the wrong we do, but also for the wrong we desire. Many an one is passing for a decent person who is really a moral leper. What pictures are hung on the walls of your mind? What does God see in 'the chambers of imagery'? Present-day divorce is both a cruelty and a curse. Experimental marriage strikes at the foundations of society, and of morality. Jesus defined the only ethical occasion for divorce.

And then, there is the matter of **oaths** (33-37). What is here in view is, not oaths as expletives, but as assurances of truth. It is here shown that everything derives its importance from its connection with God; *heaven, earth, Jerusalem,* our *heads.* In the common intercourse of life we should not use an oath at all. A man's word should of itself be the simple truth. Oaths lead men to think that there are varying degrees of truth, and the thought is morally hurtful.

Then, there is **retaliation** (38-42). What is enjoined is the readiness to renounce rights, that we may overcome evil with good. Five illustrations are given: love overcoming the evil of insult (38,39), extortion (40), compulsion (41), the beggar's need (42a), the borrower's need (42b).

Finally, there is **love** (43-48). Here the teaching rises to a noble height. We are to love, not hate; to bless, not curse; to do good, not evil; to pray, not persecute; and that for our enemies. Only so are we truly the children of the Father.

Thought: Aim at reality, not at semblance.

Against hypocrisy

In this portion are three paragraphs, and each is a warning against the sin of hypocrisy, in the matters of *alms-giving*, *praying*, and *fasting*; and in all other things for that matter.

1. **Alms-giving** (1-4). We are here warned, not against doing good, but against doing it from a wrong motive. It is right to help others, but not that we may be seen and praised of men. These people get what they go in for: their reward is having glory of men — just what they sought.

2. **Praying** (5-15). Here, avoid two things, ostentation (5,6), and vain repetition (7,8). The virtue of prayers does not consist in either their publicity or their length: a private and short prayer may be distinctly dynamic. Prayer begins in private (6). Prayer which is weak in the closet cannot be powerful in the church. Prayer *meetings* will be of little use where there have not been prayer *separations*. Alone first, then with others. If the Father knows what we need, why should we ask him (8)? To show that we *want* what we *need*. This 'disciples' prayer' is the perfect model, including as it does, worship, confession, petition, intercession and thanksgiving (9-13). The doxology (13b), whether or not textically sound (see RV), relates itself to the triple temptation of Jesus in the wilderness. His is the *kingdom* which he then refused, and the *power* which he then declined to exercise, and the *glory* which he then would not forestall. Verses 14,15 do not teach that if we forgive our fellows God will forgive us, but that God will not forgive us if we do not forgive our fellows; quite a different thing.

3. **Fasting** (16-18). What's the use of looking sad if you're not sad. Don't get yourself up, but get yourself right.

Thought: If you appear to be what you are not, you are not what you ought to be.

Warnings against materialism

This sermon is full of solemn warnings, some of greater, and some of shorter length. Here are four.

1. **Against hoarding** (19-21). Miserliness is a sin, and so is the concentration of desire and effort upon the accumulation of wealth, even when that wealth is not hoarded. Material good is a means and not an end, and when the possession of it becomes an ambition and an aim, then, the good becomes an evil. In any case, all things perishable are exposed to moth, rust, thief and other means of corruption and destruction; but treasure in heaven is out of their reach.

2. **Against insincerity** (22,23). Singleness of purpose is light; duplicity is darkness. Sincerity is health; insincerity is disease. Some think that the reference in these two verses is to niggardliness and generosity.

3. **Against a divided heart** (24). It is impossible for one's interests and energies to be thrown in opposite directions. We are under the necessity of making a choice. Though we cannot serve God and mammon, we can serve God with mammon.

4. **Against anxiety** (25-34). This is related to two of the commonest necessities, *food* and *clothing*. But why should any of us be anxious about these? The birds do not worry; the flowers do not worry. God cares for them, and will he forget us? When it says, *'Take no thought...'*, it does not mean that we are to be careless, indolent, or neglectful, but that we are not to fret. God knows, and loves, and cares; why not believe it? The key is verse 33. Let us then, steer clear alike of *avarice* (19-24), and *anxiety* (25-34). The one is the temptation of the rich, and the other of the poor, and neither becomes a Christian.

Thought: The true life is governed by principles, not by rules.

What and what not to do

1. Fault-finding (1-6). Let it not be supposed that Christ is here condemning the exercise of the critical faculty, or is exhorting us to form no estimate of the character and conduct of others. Not that, but he is condemning the fault-finding spirit and habit. Such is *dangerous* because our judgement draws God's judgement (2); and it is *ridiculous* (4), because one with a beam aslant his eye cannot possibly squint round it to see a mote in another's eye; and it is also *hypocritical* (5), because such a spirit feigns a moral interest in others which the fault-finder has not in himself. Therefore, quit fault-finding and censoriousness. But Christ goes on to teach that while prejudice against others is to be avoided, their undisguised antipathy is not to be overlooked (6). It is worse than useless to give certain truth to certain people. The lowest are not capable of appreciating the highest. We are here exhorted to exercise moral discrimination. In some company we should be silent on some themes.

2. Prayer (7-12). Observe the large place which is given in this sermon to this subject (cf. 6:5-15). The lesson of the present paragraph is, in prayer be *simple, trustful, definite, persevering.* The exhortation is based upon family relations (11). If it is natural for a child to ask, it is natural for a father to give. *Bread* suggests necessities, and *fish* suggests luxuries. The word 'therefore' (12) introduces the *golden rule.* In verses 7 to 11 is seen men's relation to God; but in verse 12 it is men's relation to one another. The ethical teaching of the sermon reaches its climax here.

3. The two ways (13,14). Mark; the *gate* and the *way, wide* and *strait, broad* and *narrow, destruction* and *life, many* and *few, go in* and *find.* Between the gate and the goal is the way. We all are already in the one way, and we are exhorted to *enter into* the other (13).

Thought: Watch your tongue and your feet.

Character and destiny

The manifesto of the King (chs. 5 to 7) tells of three things, the last of which we now consider. These are: *the subjects of the kingdom* (5:1-16); *the doctrine of the kingdom* (5:7-29); and *the way into the kingdom* (7:7-29). Under this last are *directions* (7-14) and *warnings* (15-29). In this final section we are told what is the true test of character (15-23), and the two attitudes are illustrated (24-27).

The true test of character

● *What Christ demands is conduct, not clothing* (15-20). What's the good of looking like a sheep if you're a wolf? A tree is true to its nature. If you want grapes or figs off a thorn or thistle tree, you must first tie them on. Goodness is neither the mother nor the child of corruption. According to one's nature is one's fate. Recognition is determined by production (20).

● *The Lord requires obedience, not profession* (21-23). It is not what we *say* nor what we *do* that counts ultimately, but what we *are*. On some lips the address *Lord*, is a prayer; on other lips it is a blasphemy. It is possible to *work iniquity* in the name of the *Lord* (22,23).

The two attitudes illustrated

Now, these two attitudes are illustrated: the one by a house on the *rock* (24,25), and the other by a house on the *sand* (26,27). Up to a point lives may be compared. Here are two houses; both are built; and a storm falls on both. But at last contrasts will stand revealed. One house stood, and the other fell: the storm *beat* on the one, and *smote* the other (this is the sense of the Greek). Why? Examine the *foundations*. What matters, is not what you look like, but what you rest on. 'Other foundation can no man lay than that is laid—Christ.' Are you on the Rock? Are you astonished at Christ's authority (28,29)? That is not enough—submit to it, love it, live it.

Thought: Build in time for eternity.

Mending human material

After **the enunciation of the King's principles** (4:12 to 7:29), comes **the demonstration of his authority** (8:1 to 9:34). Here *the King presents his credentials*, in three cycles, and in five realms: the physical, the natural, the angelic, the moral and the spirit realms.

We begin with *the first cycle of credentials* (8:1-22). In this portion a leper is cleansed (1-4), a paralytic is healed (5-13), fever is stayed (14,15), and many undefined miracles are performed (16).

Rationalists may say that miracles are impossible, but the Bible says they were performed. In 1910 most people would have said that it was impossible for a machine to travel in the air at 350 miles per hour; yet, it has been done; and that is not a miracle. Folks should be slow to say what *cannot* be, especially when the worker is God.

Human suffering is sorted, and is of all sizes. Leprosy, palsy, fever, demon possession and a host of minor ailments; and all, within a very limited area, but that area is a camera-obscura in which we see the need of the world.

Well is it, first, when sinners are aware of the state of their souls, and turn to Christ for what he only can do and give. And well is it, also, when we are interested enough in one another's need to concern ourselves with one another's healing. And well, thirdly, when Jesus has mercy on us without being appealed to by us.

The leper represents the first case, the paralytic, the second, and Peter's mother-in-law the third. In connection with each of these miracles is definite instruction: in the first case *ceremonial* (4), in the second *spiritual* (10,13), and in the third *sacrificial* (17). Christ was not a conjuror, but a Judge, not a sensationalist, but a Saviour. He came, and died, and lives again to deliver the whole man, the whole woman, body and soul; but his favour must be met by our faith (10).

Thought: Christ's consulting hours compass the whole clock.

Two sea scenes

It should be observed that Matthew's record does not follow chronological order, but a plan of classification. In our present division, chapters 8 and 9, miracles are brought together in order to demonstrate Christ's authority and power as the messianic King. Three particulars claim our attention here.

1. **Two would-be disciples** (18-22). The first of these was *ignorant* of what the life of discipleship involved (19,20), and the other was *insensible* of the imperiousness of the Master's claims: both went away from Christ, but by different roads. There are many paths to hell, but only one to heaven. Jesus is the Way. We need not be surprised if the severest penalties are attached to the highest privileges. The Christian life is not a picnic, but a pilgrimage (20); and its responsibilities are not optional, but obligatory (22). When duties conflict, the lower must give way to the higher. Here, for the first time in this Gospel, occurs Jesus' favourite name for himself—*the Son of Man* (20).

2. **Disciples in a storm** (23-27). Here begins *the second cycle of credentials* (8:23 to 9:17). Surely here two things must impress us: first, that fishermen should be so afraid in a gale, and second, that they should think that Jesus could save them (25). How did they expect him to do it? Had they any underlying suspicion that he was more than he appeared to be? Wretched indeed is he who is in a storm without Christ. Better a sleeping Christ than a wakeful devil. But Christ is not asleep, and that the devils know right well, as witness these—

3. **Demons exorcised** (28-34). Oh, the tragedy of some prayers answered (32,34, ch.9:1)! And oh, the mercy of some prayers unanswered! Before you entertain hard thoughts of God, think again.

Thought: Deliverance (26) or destruction (32)? These are the alternatives.

Forgiven and following

● **The palsied healed** (1-7). The state of this man's body reflected the condition of his soul, and of every unforgiven soul; they were under no proper control. Men at all times are in danger of falling into one or other of two errors: on the one hand, the care of the body, and the neglect of the soul; and, on the other hand, the care of the soul and the neglect of the body. But let us ever remember that Christ claims the whole man and woman, and neither the body nor the soul is the whole. Man is a soul and has a body, not, is a body and has a soul; and the relation between soul and body is very intimate. The ultimate significance of the body is seen in that Christ himself took it, in the incarnation.

Now, the divine ideal for the body is *health*. Christ was never sick. This is not to say that sickness cannot be in the providence of God, or that it is always due to the sin of the sufferer. Not at all. Yet, when God's purpose for his people is accomplished, we shall enjoy eternal physical health. Christ, who made many well, never made anyone ill. Think about that. It were, however, better to have a healthy soul in a sick body, than a sick soul in a healthy body: but, of course, it is best, if God so permits, to have a healthy soul in a healthy body. Get rid of your sins and take care of your body.

● **The capture of a tax-gatherer** (9-13). Suppose that Matthew had not responded when he was called (9)! We would never have this Gospel record. Try and think of the vast √ amount of good that has not been done, because men and women have refused to follow the Saviour! Only in Christ can we *realise* all that we are capable of. To invite someone to dine with you may be an introduction to Jesus (10). Ye sick, resort to the Physician. Ye righteous, bend your knees (12,13).

Thought: The feast is for the follower.

Men, women and children

● **The men**. After the scene of feasting (10) comes *a question on fasting* (14-17). It's all right to ask questions; he who never asks will never know. Shun smug ignorance as you would a plague. For every honest question Jesus has an answer. The spread table is not a feast unless the Saviour is there. Bread and water supplied by his hands are more satisfying than all the sickly luxuries of the devil's table. Our Friend's presence makes the feast, and when he is not with us, well may we fast (15).

The conjunction of Jesus and John's disciples accounts for the teaching of verses 16, 17. Judaism was passing: Christianity was coming. The *outward* aspect of the subject is illustrated by *the patch on the garment*; and the *inward* aspect, by *the wine in the skins*. Christianity is not a patched-up Judaism. On the contrary, Christianity is so new and energetic that if, as wine, it is put into the old and weak skins of Judaism, it will burst them. The new truth must find expression and embodiment in new forms. This is characteristic of Christianity in each generation.

● **The child**. Now begins the third cycle of Christ's credentials (9:18-34); *a girl comes back* (18,19, 23-26). Three persons, at Christ's bidding, came back to this world, but none of them has told us anything of that other world to which they went. Until Christ draws aside the veil, we should leave it alone. The ruler said that his child was dead (18); Jesus said that she was *not* dead (24); but by that he meant that *she was not gone for ever. Sleepeth* means neither that the breath was still in her, nor that the soul was asleep. The facts of the story interpret the words in which it is told.

● **The woman**. *Faith and the fringe* (20-22). A shrinking faith is better than no faith. This woman's purposeful touch was rewarded with Christ's personal testimony.

Thought: Christ has conquered disease and the grave.

Blind and dumb

These two miracles may seem tame after the raising of the dead, but surely they teach us that one may have life and yet be sadly defective. The dead represent this sinner in his sins, but the defective represent the saint in his short-comings. Of course the dead can neither see nor speak, but neither may the living. Christ calls each of his people to *vision* and *witness*; but all have not the former, nor perform the latter. The possession of life does not carry with it the proper functioning of our faculties.

● **The blind.** How many Christians are *blind* (27-31)! They are keen on temporal good, but careless about godliness; they eagerly pursue material gain, and easily pass by eternal glory; they know a lot about stocks and shares, but little value their soul and the Saviour. They have sockets, but not sight. Let all such cry, as did these men, 'Have mercy on us.' Do you *believe* that he who saved you can make you see (28)? Then, *according to your faith be it unto you*, this very hour (29).

● **The dumb.** But some who see do not *speak* (32-34). They have a dumb devil; their tongue is tied; their silence is sinful. What's to be done with them? Open your mouth and let the devil out. Why imprison him behind the bars of your teeth? It is wrong to speak when Christ enjoins silence (30,31), but it is sinful to be dumb when he bids us declare. May there be the noise of fleeing demons at all our prayer-meetings, and open-air services.

After **the enunciation of the King's principles** (4:12 to 7:29), and **the demonstration of his authority** (8:1 to 9:34), comes **the promulgation of his message** (9:35 to 11:30). Here, we shall consider the *need*, the *call*, the *charge*, and the *difficulties*. The *need* is set forth in verses 35 to 38.

Thought: He who sees Christ should tell of him.

On the way with the Word

The promulgation of his message (9:35 to 11:30).

● **The need** (9:35-38). Jesus' ministry was threefold: *teaching, preaching* and *healing*, which tell of the interpretation, application, and illustration of his message (35). With what vividness does he present the situation—*shepherdless sheep; labourless harvests* (36,37)! Contemplate this situation until you are driven to your knees to *pray* (38). Are not most Christians guilty of a criminal ignorance of the world's need of Christ?

● **The call** (10:1-4). All the apostles were, like their Master, young men. What a study in personality is here! Who could have imagined that that fraternity represented the future universal church of God! Not everyone can see the oak in the acorn, but it is there. All through life let us be trying to see the possibilities of things, and the potentialities of people, and we shall make great discoveries.

● **The charge** (10:5-42). The first part of this commission (5-15) relates to the days when the apostles were preparing the way for the earthly labours of their Lord, and many of these directions were purely temporary. The Lord instructs them relative to *the scope of their mission* (5,6); *the content of their message* (7); *the form of their ministry* (8); and *the principles of their movements* (9-15). Then, it was, 'Go to Israel only'; now it is, 'Go into all the world'. Then, it was, 'the kingdom of heaven'; now it is, 'the gospel of God's grace'. Then, it was with physical signs; now it is with invisible realities. Then, it was, 'If you're not welcomed, leave'; now it is, 'If you're not wanted, stay.' But both *then* and *now* are alike in this, that accountability is according to opportunity (15). Every Christian is an apostle, one sent. Have you gone? Even across the street? His is the power, but yours are the feet.

Thought: Better die serving than live sleeping.

There is trouble for the true

Under **the promulgation of the King's message** we are still considering *the charge* (10:5-42). In verses 5-8 we observe *the sphere and nature of the mission*; in 9-15, *the personal equipment of the messengers*; and now the Master tells his disciples of *the inevitable persecution*, and what should be their *attitude* towards it (16-23).

Two things here should be carefully marked; first, that this description is not of universal and age-long application, for Christ's messengers have often been in graver danger from the friendship of the world than from its active opposition; and second, though these words had a fulfilment in the period immediately following Christ's life on earth, they are to be finally fulfilled when the Son of man shall come again (23), though, of course, in a general way they are descriptive of the opposition which the Christian church has encountered all along, when faithful to her Lord.

Look at the figures in verse 16: *sheep, wolves, serpents, doves*. Sheep are mentioned for their *helplessness*; doves, for their *simplicity*; wolves, for their *ferocity*; and serpents, for their *subtlety*. Verses 16,17,21,22, are a solemn indictment of human nature. As long as such things as these are possible, there is something radically wrong with the human heart, and nothing can put it right but the Christian gospel. But, the Christian has the Triune God with him, Father, Son and Spirit (20,22), and so we can and should *endure* for our trials shall have an *end* (22).

The last part of this commission tells of *the conditions and reward of true discipleship* (24-42). The first exhortation relates to *fear* (24-31), and three reasons are given why we should not fear. First, because persecution follows almost inevitably from our calling (24-27); second, because man's power to injure us is very limited (28); and third, because all the time the Father is caring for us (29-31).

Thought: Only life can breast the tide.

The standard is set

Christ says to his disciples, *fear* me (28), *confess* me (32), *love* me (37), *follow* me (38), and, if necessary, *die* for me (39). It's a great command, and it is an astonishing claim. Think for a moment of the *claim*:

● Of God he says, *My Father* (32,33), never including others with himself, as he bids us do in chapter 6:9.

● Love for, and loyalty to, him must take precedence over all other loves and loyalties (37).

● He that follows him to the death shall live forever (39).

● They that receive him receive God (40).

Try to imagine anyone else speaking like that. All the utterances of this man have behind them the consciousness that he was also God, and it is just because he can make such claims for himself, that he can issue such *commands* to us. Consider these:

● We are to confess him everywhere and always (32,33).

● We are to be true to him, no matter what it costs (34-39). In verses 34-36, the result of Christ's mission appears as the object; and the effect as their aim. The universal and unalterable condition of Christian discipleship is that we shall in everything, everywhere, and always put Christ *first* (37-39). Test yourself by that. Is there anyone, or anything that you are putting before Christ? Think! No doubt this is a severe standard, but it is his, and by it we stand or fall.

If Christianity were so easy as to attract everybody, and so comprehensive as to include everybody, what would be the use of it? We can sacrifice too much for comprehensiveness. Christianity without its severity would be a mere sentiment, without its exacting claims it would only be an empty challenge. Are you worthy of him (37)? You will be, if with fleet foot, you follow after him at all costs. Why not? Every true follower will recognise and help every other follower (40-42).

Thought: Christ makes heroes of his people.

John the Baptist

Having considered the *need* (9:35-38), the *call* (10:1-4), the *charge* (10:5-42), we are now told of some of the *difficulties* to be encountered in the **promulgation of the King's message** (11:1-30). The attitudes of men towards Jesus are many. Here are four. First, the attitude of the *concerned* (1-15); second, of the *critical* (16-19); third, of the *careless* (20-24), and fourth, of the *child-like* (25-30).

● **The concerned** (1-15). *The Baptist represents these.* First, John enquires of Jesus (2-6), and then, Jesus witnesses to John (7-15). The bravest and most devoted have their dark days and times of misgiving. In John's question (3) we may discern both hope and fear. Never be afraid to ask an honest question

What answer did Jesus give? The answer of his works (5). Verbal claims are of no use except as they are substantiated by virtuous deeds. Christ's miracles on men showed that he was the messianic man. Is he a stepping-stone or a stumbling-block to you (6)?

So far from blaming John for his inquiry, Jesus bears witness to his weight and worth. He was neither *fickle* (7), nor *indulgent* (8), but was a *prophet*, and *more* (9); the last and greatest of the old prophetic order (10,11). 'The smallest of the truly great is greater than the greatest of the little.' In the matter of privilege the least saint in this dispensation is greater than the greatest in the last dispensation. The difference is determined by the distance of the gospel from the law.

With verse 12, compare Luke 6:16, and with verse 14, compare Matthew 17:10-13. Scripture is the best commentary on Scripture. What is the use of having ears if we do not hear (15)? Yet, alas, how often that gateway to the soul is closed when it is the truth that would enter!

Thought: Better be a true follower than a false leader.

Types of people

In relation to the claims of Christ, various attitudes are assumed. We have considered that of the **concerned** (1-15). Now look at the other three.

● **The critical** (16-19). The whimsical humour of some people is very difficult to endure. The sermon does not touch life, they say, or else, it is too straight. The preacher is not sociable, or else, he makes himself too cheap. Neither jubilance nor mourning suits them (17), and neither fasting nor feasting (18). What are we to do with people like that? See that you are not one of them. Attention is now called to:

● **The careless** (20-24). This is a sad and solemn utterance. To see holiness, and yet not repent; to live with the Saviour, and yet continue to sin; to feel the light, and yet follow darkness — that is fatal (20). Jesus here teaches that responsibility is in the measure of privilege (22,24). All shall not be judged alike, for all have not had the same opportunity. Sodom and Gomorrah were guilty, but not as guilty as Capernaum. Tyre and Sidon must answer for their sins, but their sentence will not be as heavy as that on Chorazin. It is a solemn thing to have heard Moses, but much more solemn to have heard Christ. That may be said of unbelief which Holmes said of bigotry — it is like the pupil of the eye; the more light that is poured upon it the more it contracts. Be *concerned*, but not *critical*, and not *careless*, but see to it that you are numbered among the next group.

● **The childlike** (25-30). In this paragraph are, *an acknowledgment* (25,26), *a declaration* (27), and *an invitation* (28-30). Each is momentous. Only ten prayers of Christ's are recorded, and this one is the first in order. Verse 27 is a plain claim to deity. The last paragraph is one of the sweetest in the New Testament.
—Have you *come*?
—Are you *learning*?
—Will you *take*?

Thought: Why be a serpent when you might be a dove?

What about Sunday?

We now enter upon the last section of the second division of this Gospel: **The purpose of the King** (4:12 to 16:12). 1. **The enunciation of his principles** (4:12 to 7:29). 2. **The demonstration of his authority** (8:1 to 9:34). 3. **The promulgation of his message** (9:35 to 11:30). And now: 4. **The opposition to his claims** (12:1 to 16:12). This opposition we see *in its commencement* (12:1-50), *in its consequences* (13:1-52), and *in its culmination* (13:53 — 16:12).

Here we see Jesus in controversy with the authorities.

● **The Sabbath question** (1-8). This question is as new as it is old. Have you answered it for yourself? If, for a man, the Sabbath is just a matter of rule and ritual, he might just as well play tennis and golf; but if it be a matter of spiritual worship and work, he is justified in using the means which best promote those ends. Jesus said his disciples were *guiltless* (7,cf v.1). Beings are greater than institutions. This does not mean that institutions are worthless. You who, instead of going to church on Sunday, take your family for a run in the car, or go on a picnic by rail, are not only leading your family astray, but are helping to pull down the nation.

● **The Sabbath question again** (9-21). We were taught that the works allowed on the Sabbath are those 'of necessity and mercy'. Well, eating the corn was *of necessity* (1), and healing the impotent was *of mercy* (10). Some people pay more attention to their sheep than to their own and other people's souls. Here are people who would *destroy* (14) a man for having *healed* a fellow (13)! That is a tragic factor in human nature. Jesus never aimed at popularity (16). At best it is a fickle thing. The people who lionised him one day, crucified him the next. How great are those final words — *victory* and *trust* (20,21)!

Thought: Be a benefactor, not a bear.

Blasphemy

● **The unpardonable sin** (22-32). The occasion of this discourse was the healing of a demon-possessed man (22). Opinion was always sharply divided about Jesus (23,24), but whatever yours may be, he knows it (25a). What nonsense some people talk (24)! How could Satan cast out himself? Self-preservation is one of the deepest of human instincts, and may be seen in the individual (26), the house, the city, and the kingdom (25). Beelzebub does not ill-treat his own demons; so far from sending them adrift, he finds quarters for them. What these Pharisees said was nonsense; but it was worse, blasphemy. How is that? Because they said that the Holy Spirit was the devil (24,28,31,32).

Here Jesus plainly declares the *personality* and *deity* of the Holy Spirit, for no one can blaspheme an influence, or a principle. Furthermore, he declares that he wrought his wondrous deeds by the Spirit.

Here we are face to face with the mystery of the Trinity, and the relation of the Persons (28): *I, God, Spirit*. Mark carefully these passing comments of the Master's (20,33,36,37). Everyone is either with or against him; there can be no neutrality. Root and fruit agree. What comes out of the mouth reflects the state of the heart (24). Have you ever thought how much God will forgive (31)?

Read what James has to say about the tongue (chapter 3). Guard against *idle words* (36). By our words we can bless or break hearts. When we speak we should remember that there is a *day of judgement* to come (36). How simple and how searching is all that Christ says! There is a tone of finality about his utterances. God said, '*This is my beloved Son, hear ye him.*' Listen!

Thought: Attitudes are indicated by utterances.

Sign-seeking sinners

● **The prophet and the king** (38-45). The demand for a sign was a cruel and studied insult. It reflected upon the miracles already wrought; it implied that Jesus lacked credentials; it intimated that he was making claims he could not vindicate. However, it is echoed today by men who claim that they have not proof enough for believing in Christ, or are asking for evidence of some different kind to justify their unbelief. There are signs enough to hand for those who want them.

Mark carefully the three references which Jesus makes in this connection: one is to the future (40), and two are to the past (41, 42).
—Two relate to Jonah, and one to the Queen of Sheba.
—In one, Jesus is compared with Jonah (40), and in another, he is contrasted (41).
—In one, he claims to be the greater *prophet*, and in the other the greater *king*.
—His words foretell his on-coming death, burial, and resurrection (40), and, far beyond that, the day of judgement (42).

Who then is he that can make such use of history and prophecy? His character and teaching ought to have been signs enough. The Jewish people were cured of idolatry when in captivity, but nothing worthy took the place vacated by that sin, and so unbelief possessed them more cruelly and completely than before (43-45).

● **Temporal and eternal relationships** (46-50). True relationship to Christ is spiritual affinity. Human ties are usually very tender and strong, but they are only for a while; but those that are of the spirit, and are rooted in the will of God, can never be dissolved.

Thought: Beware of the peril of decorated emptiness.

Teaching by pictures

In this long chapter we have **parabolic instruction concerning the kingdom**. It is in two parts: first, *the discourse on the sh re* (1-35); and second, *the discourse in the house* (36-52). In each of these there are four parables. This is a discourse of profound importance, and has received widely different interpretations. For example, there is no uniform interpretation of *the kingdom of the heavens*; and parables three and four have been given opposite meanings.

It is vital for understanding that the chapter be studied as a *whole*. Let us remember that interpretation is one thing, and application is another. My own view is, that we have here a prophetic programme of the course which the religion of Jesus Christ would run from his day unto the judgement day, definite phases and stages being indicated.

From another view-point the letters to the seven churches (Revelation 2, 3) cover nearly the same period. Some think that what is taught by these parables is chronologically continuous; others think that parables 5 to 7 are the *inward aspect* of that which is set forth as to its *outward aspect* in parables 1 to 4. Surely, in any case, we have here, not the church only, but Christendom including the church; that is, the whole field of Christian profession, real and unreal.

● **The sower.** This world movement begins with **proclamation**; in parabolic language, *the scattering of the seed*. That seed falls on four kinds of soil, three of which are unproductive, and the fourth of which is not equally productive. What this means in plain language, we shall see later, but for the moment, note the facts (3-8).

In verses 10-17, Jesus addresses his disciples only, and distinguishes them from the crowd; mark *you* and *them* in verse 11. He explains why he is speaking in *parable*. It is because thereby the truth is concealed from the culpably insusceptible, at the same time that it is suggested to the spiritually susceptible; but to his disciples he can speak in non-figurative language.

Thought: Here! Hear with your ear.

Proclamation and opposition

The disciples' inquiry (10), and Jesus' reply (11-23) did not in-terrupt the discourse to the crowd, for Mark tells us that that took place when he was alone with his disciples (4:10), which could not have been while he was in the boat by the shore (Mark 4:1). In his teaching, therefore, he passed from verse 9 to verse 24.

Between these, in the record, Jesus tells his disciples why he speaks in parables to the people (10-17), and interprets to them **the parable of the sower** (18-23). The *seed* is the word of the kingdom. The *soil* is the human heart. The *wayside, stony places, thorny soil,* and *good ground* are conditions of heart towards God. The *fowls* are agents of evil. The *scorching sun* is tribulation, persecution. The *thorns* are worldly cares. The *good ground* is the obedient and therefore fruitful hearer of the message.

As this parable must be comprehensive, I doubt not that the first soil tells of the man who *rejects* the gospel. The second tells of the man who *professes* to accept it, but in reality does not. The third, tells of the man who *actually does accept* it, but almost immediately backslides, and remains away from God. And the fourth tells of those who *really accept* the Word, and live by it fruitfully.

● And now Jesus speaks his second parable: **the wheat and the darnel** (24-30). In this, the first three kinds of soil spoken of in the preceding parable are not in view, but only the good ground, and upon this an assault is made. As this parable also is interpreted (36-43), observe now only the facts, which set forth the fact that no good goes unchallenged
— that when Christ gets to work, so does the devil;
— that one of the main methods of his opposition is by imita-tion;
— that he works stealthily;
— that we must act warily (29);
— that the matter will be dealt with at last.

Thought: Hostility is a test of fidelity.

Without and within

● **Relation**. Here we have two more parables (31-33), an historical note (34, 35), and the interpretation of the second parable (36-43). It is interesting to observe that this series of parables are related to one another in various combinations. For example, 1 and 2 are a pair (1-30); so are 3 and 4 (31-36); 5 and 6 (44-46); 2 and 7 (24-30, 47-50); also 3 and 5 (31, 32, 44).

● **Purpose**. Frequently our Lord spake two parables in order to present two aspects of one subject: for example, the old garment and the old wine-skins; the unfinished tower and the unwaged war; and here, **the mustard seed** and **the leavened meal**. The mustard seed parable presents the *outward* aspect, and the leavened meal the *inward* aspect of the same thing, however these may be interpreted.

● **Interpretation**. Some see in these parables the spread and triumph of Christianity; and others see in the one, the unnatural and regrettable development of Christianity into Christendom, and in the other, the corruption of Christianity by Christendom. As Jesus did not interpret these two parables, that is most likely to be the true interpretation which is closest to the facts of history. When that test is applied there cannot be much doubt as to which of these opposite interpretations is the right one.

● **Revelation**. From verse 35 we learn that what Jesus had said in these first four parables was a *revelation*; was truth spoken for the first time. He now withdraws from the public, and in a house continues to instruct his disciples; and first, by explaining to them the second parable (36-43).

He himself is the *sower*, the *field* is the world, the *good seed* are believers, the *bad seed* are sinners, the *enemy* is the devil, the *harvest* is the end of the age, and the *reapers* are angels. In parable seven the good and bad fish correspond to the wheat and the darnel here. In which category are you?

Thought: Opposites will be finally separated.

Purchaser and purchased

In this portion are, the three remaining parables of the series (44-50), a key-parable to the whole series (51, 52) and a note of the sad fact that Jesus' own relatives failed to understand or appreciate him (53-58).

● There is the parable of **the hid treasure** (44). Before, it was leaven that was hid (33). The *field* must still be the world (38). But who is the *man*? And what is the *treasure*? The treasure cannot be either the gospel or Christ, for neither is hid in the world; and the man cannot be the sinner, for he cannot purchase by sacrifice spiritual riches.

● But look at the next parable, **the pearl of great price** (45,46). Who is the *merchant*? And what is the *pearl*? Again, spiritual riches cannot be purchased by the sinner. A hymn says, 'I've found the Pearl of greatest price,' meaning Christ; but that cannot be, unless salvation is by works. What, then, do these two parables mean? Suppose the *treasure* is the plural aspect, and the *pearl* the singular aspect of one and the same thing; the one being *Christians*, and the other the *church*, and the man in each case being *Christ*. Certainly he sacrificed everything for her. He purchased the world to possess the church; the price was his blood. This interpretation presents the fewest difficulties.

● The seventh parable is **the drag net** (47-50), which pairs with the second parable, the one relating to the sea, and the other to the earth. The interpretation of verses 37-43, applies here. 'Things new and old' (52) may refer to the parables by the shore, and those in the house, or else, to the parable forms, and the hidden truths. We can never understand *all* (51).

Now Jesus returned to Nazareth, but he got a cold welcome. The misunderstanding of one's own people is the hardest thing to bear.

Thought: Unbelief paralyses omnipotence.

A prophet martyr

Under the opposition to Messiah's claims, we have considered its *commencement*, and its *consequence*, and are now to see its *culmination* (13:53 to 16:12).

Here is recorded *his rejection by all the leading classes*: by the synagogue at Nazareth (13:53-58); by Herod the king (chapter 14); by the scribes and Pharisees (chapter 15); by the Pharisees and Sadducees (16:1-12). In each of these sections we get first the rejection, and then, the result.

Ponder this story of **Herod and the Baptist** (1-12). The name Herod reeks with blood. Before this man, Herod the Great slaughtered the babes of Bethlehem. Then Herod Agrippa killed James the brother of John; and here, Herod Antipas murders John the Baptist. Why? Well, first, for marrying within the prohibited degree, Philip was a close relative; and then, for marrying the wife of another man. What business was that of John's? Purity, honour and righteousness are everyone's business. Each of us is a member of society, and what society does should concern us. Too many people today are hiding behind the delusion that the sin of their neighbour is no business of theirs.

Look at these:
- **Herod**, a moral degenerate, and a moral coward.
- **Herodias**, subtle, ambitious, clever, revengeful.
- **John**, simple, noble, loyal to conscience and God.
- **Salome** was just a pawn in this tragic game.

The wine in Herod drove out his wit; the drink helped on his doom. Such events as this, are an argument for a future life. Herod silenced the voice of John but not the voice of his own conscience. Better lose your head than heaven. Many a person has lost his soul at a dance.

Thought: The done can never be undone.

An impromptu picnic

Jesus here gives a fresh demonstration of his Messiahship, on *land* (13-21), and on *sea* (22-23).

The first story is generally called *the feeding of the five thousand*, but that is not correct; there may easily have been from 15,000—20,000 fed (21). Twice Jesus fed a crowd. He who would not feed himself in the desert (Matthew 4:3,4) fed others there. In doing so he proclaimed and proved that he was the Bread of life. Jesus did not believe that a full stomach could be a substitute for salvation; neither did he believe that salvation could best be presented when the stomach is empty. May we be saved from both these errors.

How impotent some people are in an emergency (15)! 'Mr. Chairman, I move that we do nothing.' Indeed! What a brilliant idea: such a man as that should move off. Real ability is tested by emergency; and so is faith.

Of course the disciples could not feed ten to twenty thousand people with five thin cakes of bread and two small dried fish. But what about Jesus? Was he not there? Never treat Jesus as though he were not there, and continue to call yourself a Christian. *'Bring them hither to me.'* The Bread which soon was to be broken by other hands, now breaks this bread for hungry mouths. Before the bread is broken the blessing is asked. Do you acknowledge God at every meal?

While Jesus did what the disciples could not do—multiply the food—he did not do what they could do—distribute it. In like manner, though we cannot save, we can and should proclaim salvation. Jesus did not give a little to all, but a lot to each; nor did he forget the waiters (20). The Lord of the universe is the great economist.

Thought: If you've nothing helpful to say, keep quiet.

The Master on the water

Mark and John also record this story, and there is no need to doubt the truth of it; unless it can be shown that 'miracles are impossible'.

The day is at an end; the disciples are on board ship on their way to Capernaum; the crowd has been sent home, and Jesus is on the mountain-top praying. The wind has risen, and the glassy waters are being lashed into angry foam. It is after 3 a.m. The boat is reeling in the turbulent sea. But on those waters Jesus walks calmly. The storm had made the disciples anxious, but this spectre makes them afraid. They *cry out*, but Jesus says, '*Cheer up*' (26,27). It is not easy to cheer up in a storm, especially at sea, but Christ brought the cheer with him: '*It is I.*'

The next incident is recorded by Matthew only (28-32). Peter's request may be regarded in opposite ways (28). It may be looked upon as pride and presumption, or as an evidence of faith and love. Anyhow, Jesus did not rebuke him for his request, but for his unbelief.

Peter's mind was divided between the object of faith and the objects of sense. It was when he saw his circumstances instead of Christ that he *began to sink* (30). It always is so. He did not go down to the bottom, but he *began* to. Are you beginning to sink in life's stormy sea? Then, cry quickly and briefly as Peter did, and the Master will save you from the sinful surge. Christ does not rebuke us for attempting too much, but for trusting him too little.

We may know who Christ is by what he does (33). As Jesus fed the crowd, then went to the mountain to pray, and then came to the troubled sea to rescue his own; so, having offered himself on Calvary as bread for the world, he is now in heaven interceding for his people, and soon he will come again and deliver us from the world. Hallelujah!

Thought: Better be in the wind than under the wave.

Ceremony versus sincerity

Here, Jesus addressed first the scribes and Pharisees (1-9), then, the multitude (10,11), and then, his disciples. The discussion with the religionists relates to the *tradition of the elders* on the one hand, and *the commandment of God* on the other hand. Jesus answers their *Why?* by his *Why?* (2,3). God said, 'Honour your parents'; they said, 'Wash your hands.' Now, it is well to be clean, but it is better to be kind.

See how these people evaded their duty: they pretended to consecrate to God what it was their duty to give to their parents for their maintenance. This, Jesus says, is *mouth approach*, but *heart alienation*. Washed hands can never compensate for an unwashed heart. That virtually is what the Master said to the multitude (10,11). What comes out of our mouth is our own, but not what goes into it. What goes to our heart, goes through our ear or eye, not through our mouth; but what comes from our heart, comes chiefly through our mouth.

Verse 11 annulled the Levitical distinction of clean and unclean. Perhaps it is this which caused the disciples' question in verse 12. In reply Jesus says, in effect, (13), 'If this doctrine plant of mine has not been planted by my Father in heaven, it shall be torn up' (cf. 13:29, Luke 17:6, Jude 12). Every false idea is doomed to be destroyed. '*Let them alone.*' It is the only way to deal with some people. We may only advertise evil doctrine by paying it too much attention.

What a picture is in verse 14! Look at them; all blind, linked on to one another, following their folly, right into the ditch, where each fumbles for himself if haply he may get out. The ingredient of humour is often dropped into bitter medicine which the Lord administers.

Thought: Ritualism can never be a substitute for character.

Blessings under the table

There are three words which we should distinguish, *knowledge*, *wisdom*, and *understanding*. What Christ was up against nearly all the time, was a want of understanding, on the part not only of the people (10), but also of his disciples (16,17). *Not yet?* After all my teaching? What a disappointment! Does he feel like that about you? What a hell the heart must be, out of which such demons can come (19)! Devilry is worse than dirt (20). No wonder that Jesus went away from all this rabble and wrangle to a quiet place (21). But he was never left alone for long.

This is a remarkable and important story (22-28). The woman was a Phoenician. Her daughter was demon-possessed. We are told now-a-days that it was their ignorance of psychology which led the people of those days to talk about demon-possession. It is more likely that it is their ignorance of demon-possession that leads people of our day to talk about psychology.

The disciples were great on *sending people away* (23;cf.14:15). The easiest thing to do is not always the best. This woman had addressed Jesus as *Son of David* (22). He acts upon the title, and tells her that his kingdom is Israel (24). His reference to *sheep* is impressive, seeing that David has been a shepherd. But this mother, who had made her daughter's misery her own, was not soon discouraged. Doing Christ homage, she cried, '*Lord, succour me*' (25).

In verse 26 the *children* are the Jews, and the *dogs* are the Gentiles. The woman accepted the seemingly harsh saying, and turned it into an argument why Jesus should help her (27). She asked not for the loaf, but for the crumbs. The pet dog under the table was entitled to them. She answered the Lord out of his own mouth, and he praised her for it (28).

Thought: Let your faith be like a limpet.

The Healer and Sustainer

From the borders of Tyre to the Lake of Galilee meant a long journey for Jesus and his disciples, but we must remember that they were hardy young men.

No doubt, as on a former occasion, this retreat to a mountain was for the purpose of rest and renewal, but now, as then (14:13), the design was frustrated, and instead of solitude they had society, instead of quiet rest they engaged in exacting ministry. And we have no reason for supposing that they were any the worse for it.

It is quite right to make plans; but these should always be supple, and subject to unforeseen eventualities. For extra service God always gives extra strength. On the other hand, we must not suppose that we should never rest because there is ever heard the cry of need: rest itself is part of the need. There is no use trying to catch fish with a broken net, or imagining that harmony can be got from an instrument out of tune.

How many kinds of need there are (30)! Faulty feet, sightless eyes, silent tongues, injured limbs, and much besides. But there is no want that Jesus cannot supply, and no ill which he cannot heal (31). Do you believe that? Have you come yourself to him? And have you ever brought anyone else (30a)?

Twice Jesus fed a multitude; 5,000 and 4,000, *besides women and children* (14:21; 15:38); the total may easily have been 30,000. It is strange that, after the former miracle (chapter 14), the disciples should still be unbelieving; but for an explanation of that, we have only to look into our own hearts. Has anyone of us ever been convinced once for all? Jesus' patience with us should lead us to be more patient with other people.

Thou bruised and broken bread,
My life-long wants supply;
As living souls are fed,
Oh, feed me, or I die.

Thought: The healed must be fed.

More evidence wanted

It is a terrible thing that Jesus' healing help stirred in others hellish hate. The Pharisees and Sadducees, parties usually violently opposed to one another, were drawn together by a common hatred of Jesus.

It was evening, and the glow of sunset was on the eastern hills. Jesus makes use of this circumstance (2,3). These enemies asked for a sign (1). That was a studied insult, for the land was ringing with the wonder of his works. But no sign in heaven, earth, or hell would satisfy people of such a spirit as theirs. It is not more evidence that people need of the reality of Christ's claims for himself, but more insight and sympathy, indeed, a new heart. There's no use arguing with a stone, or trying to theologise a stick. Light is only for the living; and love is the great interpreter. Observe, Jesus says that a sign would be given, the sign of his coming resurrection, the greatest of them all (4).

'*And he left them.*' It is a terrible thing thus to be *left*. The company somewhat hurriedly departed from the scene of the last miracle, and so the disciples had not looked to their supplies (5).

When the Master addressed them (6), he was not thinking of their food, but of his foes. In Mark the warning includes the Herodians. This triple warning should be carefully considered, because these men are the embodiments of evil principles; the Pharisees of *formalism*; the Sadducees of *rationalism*; and the Herodians of *secularism*. These sects no longer exist, but that for which they stood does. The tragedy is, that these evils have invaded the church, and in the degree in which this is true, they have displaced *reality, faith* and *worship*. Do *you* understand (12)?

Thought: There's no leaven in heaven.

The great confession

We now enter upon the third and last division of this record — **the passion of the King** (16:13 to 28:20). Divisions two and three both begin with the words *'from that time forth'*, with an introductory paragraph (4:17, with introduction verses 12-16; and 16:21, with verses 13-20).

The main parts of this third division are: **the revelation of his person** (16:13 to 17:21); **the instruction of his disciples** (17:22 to 20:28); **the rejection of his messiahship** (20:29 to 23:39); **the consummation of his work** (24:1 to 28:20).

Turning now to the first of these, let us consider, first, *the confession* (13-16). Look up Caesarea Philippi on the map, in Gentile territory, and understand why Jesus said *men*, and not *Jews* in verse 13. The popular guesses at who Jesus was, were all good, but not good enough (14). But the general now becomes the particular (15). What matters to you and to me is not what our neighbours think of Christ, but what we think of him, and what he thinks of us.

The answer of Peter constituted a crisis, and marked a new stage in Jesus' instruction of his disciples. Peter had not come to this conclusion (16) by any rational process (17). Such a confession can never be the product of logic, but only of light. Here is a full Christology; **Jesus**, *human*; **Son**, *Divine*; **Christ**, *Messianic*, or, in apostolic words, the **Lord Jesus Christ**. That the *gift* of verse 19 is not the prerogative of Peter or Pope, is clear from 18:18, where it is extended to all disciples.

Secondly, consider *the claim* (17-28): Jesus now more fully opens his heart (21), and Peter falls like an angel from heaven (22,23). What a bundle of contradictions he was! Observe the conditions of Christian discipleship (24,25); and the estimate Christ puts upon the human soul (26). There is a loss which is irrevocable.

Thought: Satan loves to trip a saint.

A vision on high

It is unfortunate that there is a chapter-break at this point, for it has led not a few to stumble over 16:28. As this verse cannot refer to the second coming, for all the apostles have been dead for over eighteen centuries, surely it refers to the transfiguration, which was, so to speak, a rehearsal of the coming King and kingdom. The only possible alternative is the establishment of the church at Pentecost. The *mountain* is more likely to have been Hermon than Tabor.

● *How amazing a gathering this was!* God, Christ, Moses, Elijah, Peter, James and John—seven: the Creator of all things; the Redeemer of the world; the representative of law; the representative of prophecy; the nucleus of the Christian church: two for the old dispensation; three for the new dispensation; one for every dispensation and God over all.

● *How Peter belittled this great occasion by want of understanding* (4)! It is like a woman at Niagara remembering that she had left her tap running at home! There are times when silence is truly golden. Learn to be a good listener. There was something to hear on the Mount (5). God's witness to his Son is taken from the *Psalms* (2:7); the *Prophets* (Isaiah 42:1); and the *Law* (Deut. 18:15), covering all the Old Testament (Luke 24:44).

● *This scene on the Mount was designed to stir faith, not fear* (6,7). But it is often easier to tremble than to believe.

● *Jesus only* (8). The stars are blotted out when the sun rises. But Jesus may be present without being seen. Shall we not pray for eye-cleansing?

● *They came down from the mountain!* Yes! None of us can stay up there for ever. The two points around which the redeeming revelation revolves are *suffering*, and *glory* (1 Peter 1:11). Here, the glory comes first (2), and then, the suffering. Now the suffering is past, and the glory is to come.

Thought: The higher you get the further you'll see.

At work again

Under **the revelation of the King's person** is first, *the confession* (16:13-16), then, *the claim* (16:17-28), and finally, *the confirmation* (17:1-21), which we are now considering.

● The mountain is for the sake of the valley (14-21). We dare not dwell for ever below, and we may not dwell for ever above. We get illumination, not for selfish enjoyment (4), but for service (14,15). Descent is not necessarily decline, but selfish remoteness is. Take your vision to the valley.

● How helpless we all are without Jesus (16)! These nine disciples could do nothing for this *moonstruck* boy, and sorrow-stricken father (14,15). The damp of the lowlands was in their souls. This lad's trouble was both *physical* (he was an epileptic), and *spiritual* (he was demon-possessed), and these two were so intimately connected that when the one went, the other went also (18).

● The disciples wanted to know why they had failed, and Jesus told them (19-21). '*A grain of mustard seed*' is used here figuratively because of its smallness. A little faith can do big things, but, of course, more faith can do bigger things. To remove mountains was a proverbial expression for overcoming what looked like an impossible task. Are you a mountain-mover? Or, are you a faith-failure? No one can unseat demons by unbelief. *Faith* made strong by *prayer* and *sacrifice* can do anything (20,21).

● For the second time Jesus announces his coming passion (22,23; cf. 16:21). Infidelity runs riot over the next story. One commentator asks us to believe that all Jesus meant was that Peter was to catch and sell some fish to pay the tax. What twaddle some people do talk! Money came out of the fish's mouth, but nonsense out of the commentator's. Jesus paid for himself and Peter.

Thought: Christ makes impossibility look ridiculous.

'Credo, quia impossibile est'
'I believe because it is impossible.'
Sir Thomas Browne

49

The second main part of **the passion of the King** (16:13 to 28:20), tells of *the instruction of his disciples* (17:22 to 20:28). Chapter 18 belongs to Capernaum, and chapters 19,20, to the journey through Perea on the way to Jerusalem. Our reading is all on one subject, which was occasioned by the inquiry of verse 1, about **the greatest in the kingdom of heaven.**

● *Observe, the disciples believed in a coming kingdom, and also believed that it would be good to have a high place in it.* So far so good. But we may desire a good thing from a bad motive: our spirituality may be very selfish. Hence the following discourse. Jesus said, *'Except ye turn'* (3). They were looking the wrong way. The spirit of the kingdom is the child-like spirit, a spirit of humility and trust (3). The height is for the humble; and here, by humility Jesus means a readiness to render any service (5).

● *It is an unspeakably solemn thing to lead anyone weak or unsuspecting into sin* (6). Rather than do that we should be willing to make any sacrifice (7-9). And we should not withhold our help (10-14). Let us beware of regarding the simple and dependent with *contempt* (10), for they are dear to God. We should not sneer at those whom Jesus came to save (11-14). Every single soul is precious to God (12), and no one who values his own soul should despise another's.

● *It is not God's will that anyone should 'perish'* (14). Have you ever weighed that word? To be lost, to be destroyed, to die is an unmitigated and unimaginable disaster, and Christ is the only security against it (11). We cannot escape our responsibility for our neighbours.

Thought: He who helps others helps himself.

Teaching on forgiveness

The case is here supposed of one who has been wronged, the warning of verse 7 not having been taken. Well, what is to be done? Not the right thing, I fear. First, the offended should go to the offender and try to straighten out the matter (15). If the offender will not respond, the offended should seek the co-operation of several others. If that also fails, the matter should come before the church of which the offender is a member. If still he is obdurate, he must be suspended or excluded from the fellowship (16,17).

When discipline is thus carefully and sympathetically administered, the decisions of the Christian brotherhood will receive the sanction of God; they will be 'bound in heaven' (18); but the guidance must earnestly be sought by prayer (19,20). By *agreement*, not *sympathy* but *symphony* is meant (Greek). Our hearts are the notes which the hands of the Master Musician plays.

Peter thinks that surely there is a limit to the forgiveness of offenders (21). But Jesus says, 'No' (22), assuming always that there is repentance (23-25). God never forgives the impenitent, and how can we? Albeit we should ever cherish the spirit of forgiveness.

The following parable is profoundly significant and impressive. Here is a man who was forgiven a debt of millions of pounds or dollars, refusing to forgive a man who owed him a mere pittance! They should show mercy to whom mercy has been shown, but they do not always do so. The greatest debt we can owe to one another is as nothing compared with the debt which each of us owes to God. If, on repentance he forgives us ours, we, on repentance, should forgive others theirs. An *unforgiving Christian* is a contradiction of terms.

Thought: The pardoned should be pitiful.

The risk of riches

Surely we cannot read without a sense of emotion verses 1 and 2 of this chapter. *Here Jesus finally departs from Galilee*, where for so long he had lived, and where so richly he had ministered. No one can say good-bye to a long familiar scene and a place to which he has given his soul, without a heart pang. Jesus travelled to Judaea *'beyond Jordan'* (1), by way of Perea, on the east of Jordan. Luke is the historian of this last journey's ministry (9:51 to 18:14).

Verses 3-12 of our chapter treat of **the question of marriage.**

The next paragraph, **Jesus and the children** (13-15), should be compared with 18:1-14. Have you brought your children to Christ? The future church is in the Sunday School. Workers among children are fashioning the next generation.

The next discourse extends from 19:16 to 20:16. It arose out of the inquiry of **the rich young man** (16-22). He was after the highest life, but was not willing to pay the price. He wanted to make sure of the next world, but not at the expense of this world (22). He kept the letter of the Law, but violated the spirit of it (20). He did not miss eternal life because he was rich, but because he valued his riches more than eternal life.

Millions of people are making their secondary things supreme. That is fatal. No one can enter the spiritual kingdom because he is rich, nor will anyone be excluded because he is rich. Everything depends on *how we relate ourselves and our possessions to Christ* (23-26).

Peter does not shine in what follows (27-30). '*We left all, and followed...*' he says (referring to 4:20). '*What then shall we have?*' Sacrifice should be prompted, not by hope of reward, but by love. All who share Christ's sufferings will share his glory. But there will be some surprises in that day (30).

Thought: It is not what we have but what we are that matters.

Justice and grace

The key to the interpretation of 19:16 to 20:16, is to be found in the interrogation *what?* (27), the declaration *verily* (28,29), the reservation *but* (30), and the illustration *For...So* (1,16).

Here is most important teaching on **the question of rewards**. Some thinkers consider that neither duty nor virtue should be connected with reward; that duty should be done, and virtue pursued for their own sake, and not for the sake of any gain at the end. But that is not the view of the New Testament, which has much to say about rewards, and allows the prospect of it to be a motive.

In our passage, two kinds of reward are distinguished; of *justice* (1-8) and of *grace* (9-15). The story illustrates the principle of the words with which it commences and ends (19:30;20:16). With the first labourers there was a definite agreement for a penny per day (1,2), but with the others, who began work at 9 a.m., 12 p.m., 3 p.m. and 5 p.m., there was no agreement. At the time of payment all received the same wage, and of this the early morning men complained (9-12).

Those who bargain in the service of Christ need not expect more than they bargain for. We should enter his service for love, not for gain, knowing that '*whatsoever is right he will give us*'. The surprise at the end should be, not that anyone receives so little, but that anyone receives so much. We are incapable of judging of desert, because ability, opportunity, and much besides, have to be taken into account, and only God can do that. His love can be trusted for surprising and unmerited reward. He will never be less than just, but he will often be a great deal more. *First* and *last* at the end of the day, are best in his unfailing care, and unerring wisdom.

Thought: His smile is eternal recompense.

Place or grace?

Jesus instructs his disciples, first, as to *their relation to spiritual things* (17:22 to 18:35), and then, as to *their relation to social things* (19:1 to 20:28). Under this last are considered: the law of marriage; the love of children; trust in riches; service and its rewards, and **the folly of worldly ambition**. We begin with the last of these.

A third time Jesus tells his disciples of *his coming passion* (17-19). Judas knew all about it. If anticipation is worse than realisation, Jesus must have suffered many deaths. But he went on with his work. If you knew that you would die tomorrow, what would you do today? You do not know that you will not die tomorrow! Then do what you would do today.

Now follows a discourse on **true greatness** (20-28). Nearly all Jesus' discourses arose out of immediate circumstances; something that somebody had said or done. We can excuse a fond mother wishing places of prominence for her sons, for family love may easily blind one to the virtues and claims of other people's children; but we cannot extend the same indulgence to James and John (20). They were members of a team in which each should have sought the highest welfare of all the others; but these two wanted to have the best seats. There is an ambition which we should cultivate, but this is not it.

Both these men were greatly honoured; one obtained a martyr's crown, and to the care of the other Jesus entrusted his mother. The best of people are liable to fall below the level of their own ideal sometimes.

Jesus teaches that greatness is to be found in service rather than in sovereignty, in renunciation rather than in rule; and he presented himself as the supreme example (25-28).

Think! He immediately illustrates his own teaching by *healing two blind men* (29-34).

Thought: Only the humble are exalted.

Sunday and Monday

After **the revelation of Christ's person** (16:13 to 17:21) and **the instruction of his disciples** (17:22 to 20:28), comes **the rejection of his Messiahship** (20:29 to 23:39).

Here are three parts: *the public claims* (20:29 to 21:17); *the final conflict* (21:18 to 22:46) and *the great indictment* (23:1-39). At Jericho Jesus was acclaimed as the **Son of David** (20:29-34); and at Jerusalem, he claims to be the **Great King** (21:1-17), the subject here.

With this passage commences the **Passion Week** and we have the account of **Sunday** in verses 1-11. On this day Jesus entered the royal city as the Messianic King, in fulfilment of prophecy (Isaiah 62:11, Zechariah 9:9). What would have happened if he had been received? The messianic kingdom of the Old Testament is a Jewish theocracy, and the prophecies of it are not being fulfilled in the Christian church of this dispensation.

If God's will is ever to be done on earth as it is done in heaven (6:10), it will have to be by the reign of Christ over all the kingdoms of the world, and nowhere is it said that that reign shall be realised by the preaching of the gospel. It is at this point that we see the absolute necessity for a Second Advent. Christ does not ask us to shout (9), but he does ask us to submit. The people who only shout will soon contradict their own shouts. Verses 14-17, follow on 1-11, and belong to Sunday.

Monday dawns and two things happen: first, *the Temple is cleansed* for the second time (12,13), and *a fig tree is cursed* (18,19); only the latter precedes the former in order of happening. Many churches today are little more than shops, and should be cleaned up, or shut up. Commerce in the church will put an end to consecration. Alas, alas!

Thought: Christ will be welcomed not by words but by worship.

Monday and Tuesday

On the **Monday** of Passion Week Jesus sealed the fate of the fig-tree on his way from Bethany to Jerusalem (18,19). He went to the Temple and turned out the traffickers whom he found there (12,13). To Monday also belongs what John only records (John 12:20-50). **Tuesday** was the busiest day in this week, and Matthew's record is occupied with it from 21:20 to 26:16; mark this please.

We are now to consider **the final conflict of the nation with Jesus**. This conflict was in four parts: and first, with the **priests and elders** – *the religious class* (21:18 to 22:14).

● *The withering of the fig-tree* (18-22) was an acted parable, telling of effete Judaism and its approaching destruction. This makes Jesus' reply next day, to the wonder of his disciples, the more surprising (20-22). The action of Jesus would interpret itself in due course (A.D.70); meanwhile thereby he gives his disciples a lesson on *the power of believing prayer*.

● *Now the priests and elders challenge Jesus' authority* (23-27). He answers their question by asking them one (24,25a). They found themselves on the horns of a dilemma (25b-27a), and so their question went unanswered (27b).

● But they got more than they asked for in *the parable of the two sons* which Jesus speaks against them (28-32). Two classes of Jews hear the divine call: the one, publicans and harlots, decline it but at last come; the other, priests and elders, accept it but do not come. 'Whether of them twain did the will of his father?' (31). It is not what we decline or profess to do relative to the gospel, but what we actually do, that matters. There is a piety which is hypocrisy, and there is an impiety which is at the gate of the kingdom. Your actions speak louder than your words.

Thought: Bastard sons are the curse of Christendom.

Hard hitting

Jesus spake three parables against those who challenged his authority (23). First, *the two sons*; second, *the wicked husbandmen*; and third, *the marriage feast*.

The wicked husbandmen. The meaning of the second parable is so plain that those against whom it was directed understood its meaning (41,45). The *householder* is God; the *vineyard* is Israel; *hedged* by the Law, expected to be productive (*winepress*), and protected from robbers (*tower*). The *husbandmen* are the religious leaders; the *servants* are the prophets; and the *son* is Christ. The parable is the history of Israel in miniature.

Mark carefully the claim which Jesus makes for himself in verse 37. He is the Son; greater than all the servants; he is God's *last* appeal to the people; and he is worthy of reverence. The soul or nation which rejects Christ has no ground for hope, for he is God's last Word.

Verses 38,39 detail again the on-coming crucifixion. Now, it is one thing to understand the truth (31), and quite another thing to take it to heart (45,46). How astonishing a thing to see the *builders* rejecting the *chief cornerstone!* The experts failed. The people who should have known, didn't know (42). Privileges despised will soon be removed (43). A fruitless fruit-tree had better be cut down, for it is wasting good earth.

But to come back to the *stone* (42,44). It is **Christ**, on whom Judaism fell and was broken (44); on whom and into whom the Christian church is built (Ephesians 2:20-22); and who, at the end of the age, will fall on Gentile world power, and grind it to powder (44, with Daniel 2). What is the relation of your soul to the 'Stone'?

Thought: Am I a disappointment to God?

Indifference and irreverence

In **Jesus' conflict with the priests and elders** there is first, the **approach** (21:18-22), then, the **attack** (21:23), and finally, the **answer** (21:24 to 22:14).

The answer is in three parts, which are parables. In *the two sons* the Gentiles are made equal with the Jews. In *the wicked husbandmen* the Gentiles are exalted above the Jews: and in *the marriage feast* the Gentiles are received and the Jews excluded. These parables, therefore, are of growing severity.

The marriage feast. In the last parable Jesus anticipates Israel's rejection of him, and the call of the Gentiles. When compared with the similar parable in Luke 14:16-24, we should observe that here it is narrated with marks of royalty which are in perfect harmony with the character of this Gospel. The first part of the parable (1-10) is directed against *indifference*: and the second part (11-14) against *irreverence*. The first tells of the exclusion of unbelieving Jews, and the second, of the disqualification of a professedly believing Gentile.

It is fatal plainly to refuse the message of the gospel; but it is equally fatal to place oneself within the scope of it and yet not be obedient to its demands. In the true church of God, all have on the garment of his righteousness; but in Christendom, the whole sphere of Christian profession, very many have not.

Two phrases in this parable we may well reflect upon.
● *'They made light of it'* (5): made light of the great invitation, and therefore of the King himself. To make light of the gospel is to incur a heavy responsibility.
● *'He was speechless'* (12). Yes, wrong never has reason on its side. No one will ever be able to justify his want of faith in God.

Thought: Royal guests must conform to royal claims.

Two more attacks fail

Here we see Jesus in conflict with two other parties.

First, with the **Herodians** — *the political class* (15-22). Here also, observe the *approach* (15,16), the *attack* (17), and the *answer* (18-22).

These people conceived an idea whereby they were confident they could trap Jesus. They began by complimenting him, and such worthy words could not have dropped from less worthy lips (16). To their question (17) they wanted for an answer a categorical *yes* or *no*, and either way they would have entrapped him. But he did not say either, 'Yes', or, 'No'.

Many questions do not allow of either answer. More often than not there is truth on both sides of a matter. God has his claims, and Caesar has his; and though the latter are not sovereign, they are not sinful (17:24-27). This purposed talk-tangle did not, therefore, come off (15).

Second, there is the conflict with the **Sadducees** — *the upper class* (23-33); also with its *approach* (23-27), *attack* (28), and *answer* (29-33).

How hypocritical it was of these men to assume a thing (28) which they denied (23)! Jesus tells them that they were doubly in error: they were ignorant of the Old Testament writings which they professed to believe, and they were ignorant of the divine power; the one was an intellectual, and the other an experimental, fault.

Jesus goes on to teach that in heaven earthly relations do not persist (30); but that personality persists (31,32).

These Goliaths (in their own estimation) came clattering to the ground before the sling of this divine David. *Such things had never entered their heads before*; no, nor after.

Thought: Nothing is so contemptible as proud ignorance.

Which? And who?

Three questions had been asked to entangle Jesus in his speech. The first relates to political and civil duties; the second concerns natural and physical law, and the third is in the realm of morals and ethics.

Now Jesus proposes a counterquestion: it embodies the supreme problem in the sphere of philosophy and religion. The question concerns the person of Christ; is he to be regarded as man or God, or as at once God and man? Where is Christ to be placed in the scale of being? Look carefully at this third attack upon Jesus (34-46).

● **The greatest commandment** (34-40). The Jews had a code of morality which was most complex, consisting of an infinite number of minute regulations and requirements. To be asked which of all these was the most important, would seem to these people a question which could not be answered. But Jesus, with startling insight and simplicity, forthwith answers it.

He always went to the heart of things. He always disentangled the absolute from the relative, and the essential from the dependable. So here. He says that the whole Law can be summed up in one word, **love**; that love operates in two directions, *towards God*, and *towards men*: and that to love God and our fellows is to fulfil the whole Law. By love alone can all moral problems be solved, and all moral obligations fulfilled.

● **Whose Son is the Christ** (41-46)? And now it is Jesus' turn to ask a question. It relates to himself. *How could David speak of the expected Messiah as both his son and his Lord* (Psalm 110), that is, as both human and divine? The points of importance to be observed are: that Jesus assumes the Davidic authorship of Psalm 110. He points out to the Jews the mystery of a familiar passage; he implies that the quotation relates to himself; that the Jews did not know its meaning, and did not discern the implication. The trappers are trapped. These Hamans hang on their own gallows.

Thought: Spirituality always beats sophistication.

Who not to follow

We begin **the great indictment** (chapter 23) with *the solemn warning* (1-12).

Having routed his foes in argument, Jesus now warns his friends against them and chiefly on two counts.

● **Their hypocrisy** (1-4). Here two things are distinguished, the *office* of these scribes and Pharisees, and their *character*. They taught one thing and did another. Now either what they taught was wrong, or what they did, so these leaders were wrong either way. But Jesus bids the people respect their office and teaching because it was divinely authorised (2,3), but, on no account, to do as they did. As it was, so it is. If the devil preached the gospel, we ought to respect his message, but we know, of course, that he does not believe or practise it. It is possible to get a good message from a bad man; alas that it should be so!

● **Their ostentation** (5-12). This exhibited itself in two ways, in their *love of prominence* and in their *love of power*. Both these have a common denominator, their *love of praise*. Here is a warning against calling and being called by titles which imply spiritual superiority and authority. For this latter there is no warrant in the Word of God. In this and other ways we have drifted from 'the simplicity which is in Christ Jesus'.

Spiritual power was never vested in denomination and drapery, but is to be found in Christlike character and self-denying service. No form of pretence is so objectionable as religious pretence, no honours so vain as arrogated honours, and no worship so soul-destroying as that which consists merely in the act. What the people want to see in the pulpit is not a wardrobe, but a man, not a religious official, but a saint and a prophet. And what the preacher wants to see in the pew is religion, not religiosity; moral earnestness, and not respectable indifference. Above all else, let us be *real*.

Thought: Be a brother, not a balloon.

Jesus is angry

In the last division of this Gospel, **the passion of the King**, are four parts. The third of these is, **the rejection of Christ's Messiahship**, in which are three sections: *the public claims* (20:29 to 21:17); *the final conflict* (21:18 to 22:46); and *the great indictment* (chapter 23). It is this last which we are now considering. It contains three paragraphs: *the solemn warning* (1-12); *the burning woes* (13-36); and *the pathetic wail* (37-39).

Jesus' public ministry began with eight *beatitudes* and ended with eight *woes*. No more terrible denunciations ever fell from the Master's holy lips. Here, indeed, we see 'the wrath of the Lamb'. Not only may one be angry without sinning, but there are times and occasions when not to be angry is to sin. This terrible indictment is directed against all pretence in religion.

● **The burning woes.** The first *woe* (13) is against *perverse obstructiveness*, 'against religious leaders who actually make men irreligious'. The second, is against *cruel rapacity* (14), against those who pilfered while they prayed. The third, is against *factious zeal* (15), fanatical party spirit, denominational exclusiveness. The fourth, is against *petty casuistry* (16-22), which is just moral stupidity, making distinctions where they do not exist. The fifth is against *frivolous scrupulosity* (23,24), which revealed an entire want of moral perspective. Fancy filtering out a gnat, yet letting down a camel! The sixth, is against *superficial devotion* (25,26). Our outward behaviour is of importance, of course, but our inward condition is of greater importance. The seventh, is against *defiling religiosity* (27,28), against polished pollution, against white-washed wickedness. And the eighth, is *feigned reverence* (29-33), the kind of reverence which builds the tombs of dead prophets while it plans to kill living prophets. How stern the rebuke which follows (34-36), and how pathetic the lament (37-39)!

Thought: Righteous indignation is an element of love.

Looking ahead

In the third division of this Gospel the fourth and last part is **the consummation of his work** (chapters 24 to 28), and it is composed of three sections: *his vision of the end* (24:1-25:46); *his passion for the world* (26:1-27:66); and *his victory through the grave* (28:1-20). It is a marvellous unveiling of things.

Look at his **vision of the end** (24:1 to 25:46). From the midst of apparent failure and disaster, Jesus quietly and calmly surveyed the ages, claiming for himself the position of continual supremacy. This is one of the five principle discourses of our Lord, recorded by the evangelists. Mark the *occasion* of it (1,2), the *questions* (3), and the *answers* (24:4 to 25:46).

In Scripture there are a number of prophetic programmes, passages in which is set forth the course which events would take for centuries to come, from the standpoint of the prophecy. This is one of the evidences of Scripture's unique inspiration.

Matthew 24 and 25 is one of these programmes, and should be read and studied as a *whole*. It is an unveiling of the age which began in Christ's time and continues until his return. Attention is called, first of all, to *the present age* (1-14), then, to *the great tribulation* (15-28), then to *the Lord's return* (29-31), and finally, to *the judgement day* (25:31-46). Between the revelation of the *coming* and the *judgement* are plain and parabolic *exhortations* (24:32 to 25:30).

The questions which Jesus answers are, *When?* and *What?* (3). In verses 4-14, he summarises the characteristics of this present age: deceptions, wars, famines, pestilences, earthquakes, offences, betrayals, hatreds, murders, iniquity, apostasy, *and evangelism*; and it has come to pass as it was foretold. The thing that religion and political idealism, and internationalism are up against all the time is *fallen human nature*. The world needs **Christ**.

Thought: Jesus did not guess; he knew.

The great tribulation

In this discourse, in answer to the disciples' question, the Lord speaks first of the *consummation*, and then of his *coming*. Relative to the **consummation** (4-28), he tells first, of the *beginning* (4-14), and then, of the *end* (15-28).

From verse 29 we learn that verses 15-28 tell of that prophetic period known as **the Tribulation**, frequent reference to which is made in the Old Testament prophetic books, and Psalms, and also in the book of Revelation. Students of prophecy know it as the latter half of Daniel's 'Seventieth Seven'. We must distinguish between the Great Tribulation and the destruction of Jerusalem in A.D. 70. The Lord's reference to the latter is not recorded by Matthew, but is by Luke (21:12-24). The Tribulation period is immediately related to the Jewish people, Palestine, and the appearance of the antichrist; but the whole world is affected. Connect verse 15 with Daniel 12:11.

That such a time of trouble as this is yet to come, is certain if the Bible is true; and the best efforts of men by means of the League of Nations, and peace pacts will not be able to avert it, human nature being what it is. With all efforts which make for world peace, I have the profoundest sympathy, but little hope, so long as God is left out of the councils of the nations. What men do, they can undo, but what God does, is done.

In verses 23-28 is a warning against paying heed to the false Christs who would appear. Distinguish between pseudo-Christs and antichrist. The former claim to be Christ, the latter opposes him. These verses (23-28) are a transition from the *consummation* to the *coming* parts of the prophecy, in which we are told what will be the *manner* of Christ's coming (27). Such a revelation is not designed merely to awaken curiosity, but to promote concern. Just because 'the coming of the Lord draweth nigh', we should examine ourselves, and prepare for his advent.

Thought: Dark is deepest before the dawn.

The Lord's return

The subject of 24:23 to 25:46 is **the coming of Christ**, wherein attention is called to, the *manner* (23-28), the *time* (29-51), and the *effect* of his coming (chapter 25).

For the *manner*, see previous comment. And now, the *time* (29-51). It will be at the close of the Great Tribulation, and, indeed, will close that period of travail. The appearance of the King will be heralded by certain signs which will leave no one in any doubt as to what is about to happen (29). The Lord's return will have opposite effects upon his foes (30), and his friends (31); sadness and gladness, wailing and worship, dread and delight. He will not come at the end as he did in the beginning, in weakness and humbly, but '*with power and great glory*'. His object in telling us this is not to move us to indulge our fancy, or enter into all sorts of speculation, but to call us to continuous watchfulness (32-51).

This is a crowded passage. First, the *certainty* of the advent is illustrated (32-35). Not more certainly do the budding trees herald the approach of Spring, than will these signs (29) the coming of the King. Then Jesus says, only the Father knows the hour of this great event (36), but when it occurs, the world will be found unready (37-39), as was the world of old when the flood came. History will repeat itself. We may anticipate the future by reflecting on the past. That day will be one of separations (40,41). Solemn words indeed are *taken* and *left*.

Now follow two definite exhortations: the first is to be *ready* (42-44), and the second is to be *faithful* (45-51), and we can be ready only by being faithful. We should *live . . . looking* (Titus 2:12,13), and *watch . . . working*. Our attitude towards our fellows is a true index to our attitude towards Christ. We cannot smite one another, and love him.

Thought: Watch for the last watch.

What happened 'in the middle of the night'?

It should be observed that 24:45 to 25:30 is parabolic. What precedes is in plain speech (24:9-44), except the brief parable in verse 32; and what follows is in plain speech (25:31-46), though 'sheep and goats' are used by way of figurative illustration. This change of presentation will become luminous if we understand the *plain* passages to have a *Jewish* aspect, and the *parabolic* passages to have a *Christian* aspect. The former appeal to the Old Testament; the latter do not: the former come out of a previous revelation; the latter belong to the mysteries of the kingdom. These three parables should be studied together. The first enjoins *faithfulness* (24:45-51); the second, *readiness* (25:1-13) and the third, *diligence* (25:14-30); and all point to the Lord's return.

The second parable, which we are now studying, *likens the Coming to a wedding feast*, a time of supreme joy. It tells us also that this great event was not to be immediate; and that when at last the time arrived, it would be unexpected. It is worthy of note that no mention is made of the *bride*. Is the *bride* Israel, and are the *virgins* Christendom? In that view all is clear. Then, the five foolish virgins are those who profess to be Christ's, but are not, because they have not the Holy Spirit (8); and the five wise, are genuine Christians, albeit when Christ comes they are found slumbering (5).

Too late the mere professor of Christianity wakes up and asks for oil, but moral life and spiritual graces cannot be divided and shared in such an hour. It will then be too late to turn for help to friends and associates. Jesus is willing to receive you now, but when he arrives your opportunity will be past. There is a universe of difference between an oil-fed torch and smoking tow. Which are you? If any man hath not the Spirit of Christ he is none of his. But, it is to be feared, many who have the Spirit are sleeping. The Bridegroom will not wait for us to wake; he expects us to watch.

Thought: Only the Spirit can prepare us for the Bridegroom.

What should happen while it is day?

The parallels between this and the previous parable should be considered: the bridegroom, and a man travelling into a far country; the virgins, and the servants; the lamps, and the talents; the wedding, and the reckoning; and, of course, the untimed return. The previous parable exhorts to *readiness*: this one, to *diligence*. The Christian should be both looking and working. To look and not to work is folly.

This parable of the **talents** should be compared and contrasted with that of the **pounds** in Luke 19. The framework of both is, the *going*, the *absence*, and the *return*: and in both the emphasis is on what is done during the absence. To each of these servants is given a trust according to his capacity (14,15): these servants are then contrasted (16-18): and then follow, the return, the reckoning, the reward of the diligent, and the recompense of the indolent (19-30).

The parable teaches that the sphere of service grows larger as we serve, and that capacity also grows with experience. In spiritual things none of us is shut up to mediocrity. The talents are the opportunities which answer to our abilities. No one has more opportunity than he has ability, and *no one has less*. The tragedy is that the man who can least afford to neglect his opportunity, because of his limited ability, is generally the one that does so.

But let it be said, no one can improve our talent for us: if we do not use it, it is not used. If we have but one talent, every day's believing use of it will carry us on some way towards two. By neglect of our talent, we lose not only the capacity for gaining more, but also the talent itself.

Learn also that faithfulness, whatever one's ability, is *equally* rewarded. The unfaithful servant is not a servant of Christ's at all.

Thought: To do nothing is a damning deed.

Sheep and goats

This is not the place for dogmatic detail of exposition, but it should be said that the general view of this passage, which reverts again to plain speech, is that it depicts *a general judgement at the end of the world*. Such an interpretation is not only inconsistent with all that has preceded in this discourse, but is also inconsistent with all the prophetic Scriptures on the subject of judgement.

There is space only to summarise my view. Chapter 24:4-44 relates to *Jews*; chapter 24:45 to 25:30 to *Christians*; and chapter 25:31-46, to *Gentiles*. The event predicted falls between the first resurrection, of saints for glory; and the final resurrection, of sinners for judgement at the Great White Throne. More closely, it is a judgement which is to take place at the close of 'the great tribulation' spoken of in Revelation 7:14, and that blood-washed white-robed multitude are the *sheep* of our passage, *Gentiles*, mark you (Revelation 7:9).

This is a judgement which follows the *coming* of the previous parables, and so the church of God is no longer on the earth (1 Thessalonians 4:13-17). The justification of those on the right hand of the Son of Man is not on the ground of their having been kind, having done good deeds, for salvation is not by works, but their deeds are the evidence of their attitude towards the Christ and the gospel of the kingdom (24:14). Actions reveal attitudes, and our conduct discloses our character.

Let no one imagine that Jesus is here teaching that eternal life can be secured by being kind to the poor, regardless of any relationship to him, and in spite of lack of moral character or faith. Oh, no! Let us learn that judgement is a solemn and certain reality, and that the return of Christ will be a time of separation among men. Whatever you think of them 'eternal life' and 'eternal punishment' are realities.

Thought: The act of our hand reflects the attitude of our heart.

Devotion and treachery

Following **Christ's vision of the end** (chapters 24,25), comes **his passion for the world** (chapters 26,27), telling of the *supper* and the *garden*, the *betrayal* and the *trial*, the *cross* and the *grave*.

One cannot but be impressed with this turning of Jesus from that vast, prophetic survey (chapters 24,25) to the tragic events of the next few days. Yet, how closely they are related. Without *this*, *that* would be impossible. Here the camera is brought nearer. In the two preceding chapters we get perspective, but here we get particularity. There, is the *circumference*, but here, is the *centre*.

Our portion presents startling contrasts. A woman, a man; a friend, a foe; giving something, getting something; devotion, deceit; sacrifice, selfishness; buying opportunity, selling opportunity; alone, in alliance; a box of ointment, thirty pieces of silver; blessed, cursed. Life is full of such contrasts as these, and they are cheek by jowl all the time. Now, as then, the counsels of God and of men are opposed (1-5); now, as then, loving discernment and hating design lie alongside of one another.

Think carefully about the *adoration* of Mary (7), the *utilitarianism* of the disciples (8,9), and the *treachery* of Judas. What a conjunction of ideas and emotions! 'To what purpose is this waste?' A thing may be morally beautiful, which is not practically useful. Christ understands the meaning and motive of what we do for him. Duty is not a virtue; virtue is a plus; it is the second mile (5:41).

Poor Judas! Are you satisfying or selling your Redeemer? Do you grudge him anything that can be done for him? Remember what he has done for you.

Thought: He will never forget your ointment (13).

Two feasts

Mark carefully the order of events here. **The Passover Feast** precedes **the Lord's Supper.** Judas was at the former, but not at the latter. He was at the last feast of the old dispensation, but not at the first of the new. No unsaved person has any right to partake of the holy sacrament, and so to do is to eat and drink condemnation.

Our portion suggests many things and teaches many lessons. Learn, that here type passes into antitype (17,26), that Jesus had many unnamed friends (18), that it is the disciple's duty and wisdom to do as he is told (19), that where Christ is, evil is always detected and exposed (21,23,25), that self-suspicion better becomes a Christian than self-confidence (22), that divine foreordination and human freedom interlock (24), that it would have been better if some people had never been born, which raises the question of the part which God has in conception (24), that the Lord's Supper is the memorial of a new covenant (28), that Jesus knew his approaching death was to be vicarious and atoning (28), that Christ's death is *on the behalf of* sinners, but *instead of* only those who believe (28), that Jesus looked beyond the cross to his triumph in a far distant kingdom (29), that song is not incompatible with sorrow (30).

The hymn was all or part of Psalms 115-118. Between verses 20 and 21 of our portion, read John 13:1-20; and after verse 25, read John 14:1 to 17:26. The disciples were depressed, but Jesus was joyful; they were full of fear, but he, full of hope; they saw an approaching calamity, but he, a mighty conquest; they looked *at* the coming event, but he looked *through* it. Blessed, spotless Lamb of God!

Thought: I am blessed because he was broken.

In the garden

It is night, and Jesus, with his disciples, leaves the upper room. They walk together by the Temple, down the slope of Moriah, and across the Kidron valley *'unto a place called Gethsemane'* (36). It is on the way to the garden that the conversation of verses 31-35 takes place. The Master warns his followers, but, led by Peter, they all protest that they would never fail him (31-35). The fault was not in their declaration of love, but in their ignorance of weakness.

At the Lord's Supper we should ever cast ourselves anew upon his promised grace, by which alone we can triumphantly face the trials of the night, and look with confidence for that morning which shall be without clouds. But this the disciples did not. Being sure of Christ, rather than being sure of ourselves, is the secret of victory.

And now they reach **Gethsemane**, and how solemnly sacred is what follows. Eight of the disciples are left within, but near the entrance. Jesus, Peter, James, and John go further together. He tells them that his 'soul is circled with grief', and asks them to watch with him (38). He leaves the three and goes still further into the garden, into the deep shadows of the olive trees, and there he prays, three times; but between each prayer he returns to the three for sympathy, but, alas, both times he finds them asleep.

What can we say about it? The safest thing is to say what he said (41). How profound a mystery are Jesus' two wills, the human, and the divine. Here his human will is yielded to his Father (39). He shrank from the cross, but he accepted it. The thing of sovereign and eternal importance to Jesus was *the will of God*. Is that everything to you?

Thought: Are you willing to go 'a little further' (39)?

The arrest

We are now to consider **the betrayal and the trial of Jesus** (26:47 to 27:26). In our present portion we concentrate on **the betrayal**.

There is first the **approach of Judas** (47-50), who is still spoken of as 'one of the twelve'. He is accompanied by a rabble of leaders and underlings, elaborately equipped, and expecting, therefore, to be resisted (47). The sin of Judas was the more heinous by reason of the way in which it was performed (48,49). To betray his Master was hellish enough, but to do so by *kissing him much* was to make a fine art of devilry. Only twice is it recorded that Jesus was kissed, the other time by a penitent woman (Luke 7:38,45): once by hate and once by love.

Judas said to Jesus, 'Rabbi', and Jesus said to Judas, 'Friend' (49,50). The word which Jesus uses (*hetairos*) is not that which he employs in John 15:14 (*philos*), but means *fellow*, or *associate*, and in none of its occurrences in Matthew does it mean friendship. See 11:16; 20:13; 22:12. Jesus never paid empty compliments.

Next we are told of **the zeal of Peter** (51-54). John tells us that it was Peter, and that the victim was Malchus, and, doctor-like, Luke says that Jesus healed him. Jesus fought might, not by might, but by right: his weapon was *truth*. Ponder verse 53. Jesus could have obtained the instant help of 72,000 angels, but had he done so, Isaiah 53, and Psalm 118:22, and much besides, would never have been fulfilled (54). But while the Master yields he *protests* (55). His whole past bearing and teaching made their display of militancy look absurd.

The Evangelist adds two brief notes; one saying that he saw in these events a fulfilment of Old Testament prophecy, the other, that in this dire hour, all Jesus' disciples, including himself, forsook him. Matthew wrote this from thirty to forty years after the event, when he had long been forgiven.

Thought: Christ expects me to be loyal in the hour of crisis.

Two men on trial

There were six phases in the trial of Jesus, three of them being Jewish or ecclesiastical, and three of them Gentile or civil. 1. Before **Annas** (John 18:12-24). 2. Before **Caiaphas** (57-68). 3. Before the **Sanhedrin** (27:1,2). 4. Before **Pilate** (27:11-14). 5. Before **Herod** (Luke 23:8-12). 6. Second before **Pilate** (27:15-26).

Our present portion tells of the second of these so-called trials, beginning at verse 57. See how it began. These religious leaders of the people sought 'false witness' *(pseudomarturian)* against Jesus. What a word! Behold the origin of this wicked thing (15:19). The moral bankruptcy of these men was complete. But even for false witness to have any force it must have in it an element of truth, as here (61); see John 2:18-22.

How composed Jesus is in the midst of all this commotion (63)! It is useless to reason with some people. The issue of this trial was determined before the trial began. What a farce! But Jesus speaks at last (64). The question of Caiaphas (63) was vital, and silence might have been taken as equivalent to a denial. The Holy Spirit will teach us when and when not, to speak.

What follows is the most shameful travesty of law (65-68). Not only was the recognised procedure departed from (66), but they indulged in vile and cruel abuse (67,68). In reality Jesus was the Judge and all these people were the criminals. Things are not always what they seem.

And now we are given a glimpse of Peter again (69-75). He had gone into the court of the palace 'to see the end' (58). He would have been wise had he paid more attention to his own end. Thrice did Peter deny his Lord, and thrice did he confess him (John 21). Poor Peter! He was as yet splendid stuff unmade; a diamond in the rough. When he came into the hands of the Spirit, a wonderful transformation took place. What about you?

Thought: To stand firm you must kneel more.

The death of Judas

The third stage of Jesus' trial is reached in 27:1,2, before the **Sanhedrin** (cf. 26:59). Only the fact is mentioned, and we are hurried on to the fourth stage, before **Pilate**, in verses 11-14. But in this reading we are asked to contemplate **Judas** (3-10). What a career, and what an end! Some bad men become good, and some good men become bad, but here a bad man remained bad to the end. His confession and remorse do not imply repentance in the evangelical sense. Peter's repentance led to sanctification, but that of Judas led to suicide.

Fancy a disciple selling his Master, and such a Master, for thirty pieces of silver! Of what use was that to him? And remember, Judas sold not only his Lord but also himself for that. What price do you put upon your soul? Some sell their souls for money quickly made, others for a mess of pottage, but Judas got nothing out of it.

Some things once done can never be undone, though one's tears were blood, and flowed like a river. In the reference to *innocent blood* there is no trace of acknowledgement that Jesus was the Christ. Probably Judas never knew that; but his ignorance does not mitigate his offence. *He hanged himself.* Compare Acts 1:18. These accounts are not contradictory, if we assume that the rope broke. The most intimate association with Christ cannot save from hell one who does not believe.

Now look at the **priests**. 'It is not lawful,' they say. Contemptible hypocrites! Was it lawful for them to have given the money to Judas in the first instance? They bought the potter's field, but they were never in the Potter's hand. The prophecy fulfilled was not Jeremiah's, but Zechariah's (11:13):probably no name was in the original account. Both Judas and Jesus died a violent death, but ethically the difference between them is the difference between hell and heaven.

Thought: Character determines destiny.

The judge judged

Here are recorded the fourth and sixth phases of Jesus' trial, the first and second appearances before **Pilate**. Between verses 14 and 15, comes the fifth phase, the appearance before **Herod** (Luke 23:8-12). In Matthew's account of Jesus' first appearance before Pilate (11-14), the impressive feature is his silence. He answered the Governor, who was acting judicially, but not the chief priests and elders, whose whole procedure was illegal. There are times when the only reply consistent with dignity and honour is silence; to speak to some people would be an humiliation.

Herod makes little of Jesus, and less of himself, and sends him back to **Pilate**; and there now follows an account of the sixth and last place of this caricature of a trial. Pilate is called the Governor, but it is truer that he was the governed and the prisoner was the Prince. Honour, wisdom, and power are not always associated with offices, titles and uniforms. The ultimate reality is character.

Pilate knows from the beginning that Jesus is innocent, yet he is afraid to do right in the present because of his faults in the past. He toys with his convictions until they no longer carry any weight; he fools with his conscience until it ceases to operate. *'What shall I do, then, with Jesus?'* It is not, 'Shall I do anything with him?' We all must do something with him, and it is only a question of *What?* And further, there is only one alternative.

Jesus and **Barabbas** stand for opposite principles, and represent opposite attitudes towards God. The choice must be made between them: between the Son of the Abba and the son of Abbas (Bar-Abbas). There can be no neutrality. Washing one's hands can never cleanse the stain from one's heart (24). Judas acknowledged that Jesus was innocent (4), but Pilate claims that he is himself innocent (24)—so completely may one deceive himself. Here is another moral ruin. The Governor is his own judge.

Thought: The alternatives are Christ's side or suicide.

Outside the city wall

With impressive brevity and clearness the Evangelist outlines the following events, showing us Jesus in the Praetorium (27-31), on the way (32), and at Calvary (33,34).

● **In the Praetorium** (27-31). See these six hundred coarse, ignorant brutes bullying a helpless, innocent Man! But their hateful jests had a significance of which they never dreamed. He was entitled to royal robe, crown, sceptre, title, and the worship of men, and will ultimately receive them. What, then was his in mockery, had always been his morally, is at present his spiritually, and soon will be his historically and eternally. What a commentary is this scene on human nature! We may never descend to such a depth as this, but we are capable of doing so. What human nature needs is not reformation but recreation.

● **On the way** (32). Now behold the scene between the hall and the hill, along the *Via Dolorosa*. Weakened by his sufferings, Jesus falls beneath the weight of the wood they had laid upon him, and, it would seem from Mark's account (15:22), the soldiers had to carry him the rest of the way to Calvary. His cross they put upon a Jew from North Africa.

When Simon rose that morning, little did he anticipate what would befall him during the day; yet he was to make history: he bore the cross which Christ was going to bear for him. How true it is that none of us knows what a day may bring forth. *You* may today find yourself in the midst of undreamed of circumstances; you may be called upon to share a bit of the world's sorrow, and to feel the throb of its aching heart. So pray before you leave the house today, and commit yourself to the Lord. It is dangerous to leave home any day without Jesus.

● **At Calvary** (33,34). The holy Victim and Vicar, is not on the cross (33,34). Why did he not take the gall-wine? Because it was intoxicating, and he chose to die with clear consciousness. For you. For me. Thank him.

Thought: Follow thy friend though the way be flinty.

The glorious, shameful cross

I confess it is difficult to write on this passage. The record of our Lord's crucifixion is so plain and poignant, and at the same time so mysterious and glorious, that to further expound it seems to be both unnecessary and impossible. This is the focus of all history; the universe centres in a cross.

This tragedy was the greatest of all triumphs; this failure was the most consummate success. Out of this darkness has come eternal light, and from this death there flows eternal life. Jesus was forsaken that we might be forgiven; he was wounded that we might be healed. If he had saved himself, he could not have saved us: had he come from the cross we would have gone to it. If he had not died there, Barabbas would have.

Those three crosses were made for three robbers, but the middle one was occupied by the Redeemer, who robbed heaven that earth might be enriched. The title on the cross is enlarged by being curtailed. Take off the last three words, and you put on the whole Gentile world. This is addition by subtraction. The Saviour prayed for those who railed on him.

God is Light, and when he turned his face away from the land, of course it was dark (45,46). When the light returned, God was looking again. From Sinai to Calvary there was a veil between earth and heaven, but when Jesus died it was for ever rent, and by God, not by man, for it was rent *from the top* (51).

More than one commentator says that what is said in verses 52, 53, is *purely legendary*; on the contrary, what such commentators say is pure infidelity. It is a less wonder that the dead should live than that the Living One should die.

Lifted up was he to die;
It is finished! was his cry;
Now in heaven exalted high;
Hallelujah! What a Saviour!

Thought: The slain Lamb has made possible the saint-life.

The sealed sepulchre

Let us consider the **grave**. Verses 55,56 belong to the previous section. The story of the burial, which covers also the time that Jesus was in the tomb, traditionally from before 6 p.m. on Friday night, until early on Sunday morning, is briefly told.

The crisis discovered **Joseph** (57,58). Why had he not appeared before? Several people of his type are introduced into the Gospel story. They represent all whose love for Christ is brought to light by difficulty and danger. If the 16th century fires of martyrdom in Smithfield, London, were lit again, probably many professed Christians would recant, but almost certainly many who have made no open confession would declare themselves; the Josephs, the Nicodemuses, the upper-room owners, and donkey owners of the church. But why not declare yourself now? Why keep your testimony for the tomb?

This burial of Jesus was the fulfilment of prophecy. '*They assigned him a grave with wicked men, but with the rich man when he had died*' (Isaiah 53:9; Hebrew).

Mary is the sweetest of all women's names because of its sacred associations. It was the name of Jesus' mother. When the men fled, the women followed (61). The lot of Jesus would have been harder but for the love of certain women who ministered to him in many ways. Are you a joy or grief to the Lord? Are you helping or hindering?

What Jesus' friends should have hoped for, his foes feared, namely, that he would rise from the dead (62,63). Is not that an impressive fact? They felt that the spread of the resurrection claim would be worse than the spread of the messianic claim (64). Observe the occurrence thrice of the word *sure*; as though anything could be sure that is opposed to God! They could seal the stone, but could not stay the Saviour. How foolish is man's wisdom, and how impotent his power!

Thought: Christians should not fear the grave.

Risen and seen

Review for a moment the **consummation of Christ's work** (chapters 24 to 28): *his vision of the end* (chapters 24,25); *his passion for the world* (chapters 26,27); and now, *his victory, through the grave* (chapter 28). This last tells of his *resurrection, manifestation,* and *commission.*

Consider then, **Christ's resurrection** (1-7). This is an amazing story. It is not a record of the rising, but of the resurrection. In order to promote faith it was not necessary that anyone should see Jesus rise, but only that the risen One should be seen.

This is an angel's story, and it reveals to us a lot about angels. They are embodied, and can freely pass from heaven to earth (2). This angel had on clothes, was dazzlingly bright, and struck terror into those who saw him (3,4). He spoke, presumably in Aramaic, for he was understood. What the watchers did, he bade the women do not (4,5). He knew Jesus, and knew for what the women were at the grave (5). He knew that Jesus had predicted his resurrection, knew that he was risen, told the women so, and bade them examine the place (6). He calls Jesus 'the Lord'. He knew that Jesus had disciples, bade the women tell them of the resurrection, informed them that Jesus would appear to them in Galilee, and speaks with the note of authority (7). This is a momentous contribution to biblical angelology. Think about it!

Now follows, **Christ's manifestation** (8-17): and first of all to these faithful women. See them running, and contemplate their mingled emotions, *fear* and *joy* (8). Then, what a surprise! He himself appeared and spoke to them. They knew him, laid hold of his feet, and worshipped him. What a moment! Jesus bids them part with one of their emotions, but not the other (8,10). For the first time he calls his disciples *brethren*, and promises to meet them (10). Do you feel the thrill of all this in your own soul? His resurrection is a power as well as a fact.

Thought: Only they who have eyes can see.

Risen and ruling

What opposite effect the same event can have upon different people! What made the women thrill with joy, made the Roman guard tremble with fear (11-14). To the latter the empty tomb spelt disaster, but to the former, it spoke of dayspring. The event was the same, but the people were different. What Christ is to anyone depends upon that one's attitude towards Christ.

The story which these elders hatched was as risky as it was ridiculous, for what business had the guard to be *asleep* (13)? But Pentecost was not the product of a stolen body. It may be difficult to believe that Jesus rose from the dead, but it is more difficult to believe that he did not. The witnesses are too many and varied to allow of any doubt, if testimony counts for anything. Some of these might have been deceived, but not all of them, and all the time. Moreover, what Jesus was and did, make the miraculous conception and the resurrection not only possible, but necessary.

But beyond the resurrection, and because of it, is **the great commission** (18-20), the note on which this Gospel ends. How comprehensive it is, *all nations*; how commanding, *all authority*; how exacting, *all things*; and how satisfying, *always*. The divine order is: *Go, make disciples, baptise, teach.* What is the prevailing order today? Go, baptise, Christianise and don't teach! The Christian religion is essentially *missionary*, it must spread. If you have a gospel which you do not think it worthwhile to give to someone else, you might just as well be without it yourself. Christ's vision was always age-long. He always had in view far-distant ends.

If Jesus did not rise from the dead, we have to account for the Christian church throughout nineteen centuries. So ends the tax-gatherer's record of his Master's career.

Thought: Virtue of character gives value to service.

Mark's Gospel

Contents

Mark's Gospel

Although the Gospel does not refer to its author it was un-doubtedly written by John Mark, the son of Mary, who lived in Jerusalem (Acts 12:12). He was a cousin of Barnabas (Colossians 4:10) and possibly had been converted through Peter (1 Peter 5:13) whose eye-witness account of the life of Jesus he faithfully records. Peter's influence is seen, for instance, in the fact that the Gospel begins with his call to discipleship and there is no mention of the nativity.

Mark's Gospel is among the earliest New Testament writings and might be dated between A.D.50 and 60. It may have been written in Rome, and certainly it appears to have been prepared principally for Roman readers. There are few Old Testament quotations, and words which Romans would not have understood are translated (3:17; 5:41, etc.), while Jewish customs are explained (7:3,4).

The narrative is full of action with emphasis on deeds rather than words, and extended passages of teaching are not found as in the other Gospels. It is an artless, compelling record of the ministry, death and resurrection of Jesus.

The worker on the way

As we study this record I intend, by observations and interrogations to call your attention to the text of the Gospel, and to your own life in the light of its truths.

Let us begin by getting a comprehensive view of the whole book. It is a portrait of **Jesus the divine worker** and we are shown *his life's day of work*. In 1:1-13 we have *yesterday*. In 1:14 to 15:47 we have *today*. In 16:1-20 we have *tomorrow*. The *today* portion is central, with a glimpse of the *preparation* the day before, and the *exaltation* the day after. These *days*, you will observe, are periods of time. The first was about thirty years; the second about three and a half years; and the third, eternal years.

Today (1:14-15:47) is presented in seven pictures: 1. *Dawn or acclamation* (1:14,15); 2. *Morning or opposition* (2:1 to 3:6); 3. *Forenoon or separation* (3:7 to 6:13); 4. *Noon or consummation* (6:14 to 8:26); 5. *Afternoon or education* (8:27 to 10:52); 6. *Evening or condemnation* (11:1 to 13:37); 7. *Night or crucifixion* (14:1 to 15:47).

This is an outline of *Jesus' day of work for the redemption of the world.* Keep the picture quite distinct from that of the King in Matthew, the Man in Luke and the Son in John. Here he is the Servant, and the servant works.

Our present portion treats of **yesterday** (1:1-13), and tells of *preparation* for tomorrow, and the day after. Between the *preparation* and the *exaltation* comes the *ministration*. It is always the order. There is no worthy ministration where there has not been prolonged preparation; and there is no true exaltation unless there has been sacrificial ministration.

Thought: Take time to get ready.

Attraction and repulsion

Here **the day of work** begins and it is **dawn** or **the acclamation of Jesus**. We are shown at once that this person and work had the power to *attract* (14-20) and *repel* (21-28).

Men followed and demons fled.

When John went off the scene, Jesus came on (14). God never leaves himself without a witness. In God's eternal purpose there is a *time* for everything; he never is before his time, and never is behind (15a).

No one can *believe* who does not *repent* (15b). These men were at work when Jesus called them into his service (16,17): the best preparation for coming tasks is present toil. He who would *become* must first *come* (17). Why try to make yourself when Christ has offered to *make you* (17)? What is worth doing should be done *straightway* (18). The Christian sequence is *repent, believe, forsake* and *follow* (15,18).

It is good when whole families follow Christ (16,19): are all your family following? Mark, Jesus did not call Zebedee (20): everyone cannot be a minister or a missionary, but we can all serve Christ where we are, and somebody must look after *the hired servants* (20). He whom you will find *by the sea*, you will find also *in the city* (16-21); happily for us there is no escape from him. Jesus went to church on Sunday; do you (21)? The modern outcry against *authority* in religious matters is really a challenge to Christ (22-27).

It was when Christ's *teaching* began to take effect that Satan came into action; it always is so (22,23). Demons also go to church (23); see to it that you are never their conveyance. Observe that these demons knew who Jesus was, and knew their own fate (24), and these two things are closely related. When evil spirits get notice to quit they must go, but they will do all the damage they can when they leave (26). Have people ceased to be *astonished* and *amazed* at what Christ is doing? Have you (22-27)?

Thought: To men Jesus says, 'Come'; to demons he says, 'Go'.

Sunset and sunrise

This writing being the record of **the divine servant**, it is his works and not his words which dominate the narrative; his tools rather than his teaching; his doings rather than his doctrine; and so there passed before our eyes, as on a film, a rapid review of his many and multiform activities.

This first chapter of the narrative is typical of the whole. We see Jesus alone (35), and with others (38), at work in city and by sea, in synagogue and home, calling in men and casting out demons, helping and healing, teaching and praying.

Study in detail each of these characters: **Simon, Andrew, James** and **John**. Which of these wrote Holy Scripture? Which of them died a martyr's death? Which of them lived the longest? Which of them knew Jesus best? Which of them was related by birth to Jesus?

Never let us forget that we are saved to serve: she who was *lifted up, ministered unto them* (31).

Jesus did wonderful things at *sunset* (32). At the end of each day, before the night enwraps us, we ourselves should come and should bring others to our Lord for deliverance from all their diseases (32-34).

The test of a man's reality, the revelation of his character is in what he will do when he is popular (33), in how he will react to the acclamation of the crowd. What did Jesus do (35)? The only right and safe thing to do is to go from the throng to the throne, from preaching to prayer. No man who is not often alone with God, will last long before men.

Between verses 39 and 40 comes the *Sermon on the Mount* (Matthew 5 to 7), a sample of the *preaching* spoken of in verses 38,39. Mark the sense of urgency in Jesus' ministry by the occurrence of the words *straightway, immediately, anon* in this chapter, and throughout the Gospel. Are you busy for God?

Thought: Use the sanctuary of solitude.

A hole in the roof

Here the **dawn** gives way to **morning** and **acclamation** to **opposition**.

Jesus ennobled Bethlehem by his birth, Nazareth by his labour, Capernaum by his residence, and Jerusalem by his death. Indeed, in some way, he enriched every place he entered. Can this be said of us? Some people pollute the air as they pass, and some sweeten it. No place was foreign to Jesus: sea, city, synagogue, mountain, and house were in his world of action and nowhere could he be hid (1).

Crowds come together from various motives: curiosity or concern, antipathy or anxiety. All sorts of people draw crowds—bishops and buffoons, clergy and clowns. What counts is what one does with the crowd that gathers. Jesus *'preached the word unto them'*. He was not, like some who bear his name, a religious entertainer, but a divine instructor: he gave the people food, not straw.

See, here are some kind folks who want a palsied fellow healed, and they *'could not come nigh unto Jesus for the press'*. But these folks were not to be beaten: if they could not get in one way, they would another. Alas, too many well-wishers are wholly lacking in enterprise and ingenuity. Why cannot we Christians do something original to get men saved? Before many churches see revival, their roofs and walls of conventionality will have to be broken up, and broken down.

'Jesus saw their faith.' He always sees it where it exists, however little or weak it may be. Of course there was never a congregation where there was not a critic, and here we see that criticism begins in the heart (6). *Why? Who?* But the other side can ask questions also. *Why? Whether?* The scribes' questions were born of ignorance, the Saviour's of knowledge. It is equally easy to *say* both these things (9), and equally difficult to *do* either of them; but Jesus both *said* and *did*. The man rolled up his mat and went off home. Wonderful!

Thought: Is your mat under your back, or under your arm?

The rumbling of grumbling

Jesus did by the sea (13) what he had done in the house (2), and *the whole multitude kept coming to him.*

It was at this time that he saw a man, Levi, *sitting at the toll office*, collecting Roman taxes. All Jesus said to him was, '*Follow me,*' and he did! Behind that swift action of his is a story which is not told. We have just read of a man sick of the palsy; here is a man sick of his occupation. If you are not in an honest business, get out of it: hear Jesus say to you, '*Follow me,*' and go right away after him for he is *passing by* (14).

Later, this converted tax-gatherer expressed his gratitude to his Saviour, and also his concern for his fellows, by inviting Jesus and his disciples (four at this time) to a feast, together with '*a large number of tax-gatherers and sinners*'. He must have been well-to-do. What a setting for the Saviour!

I'm certain the time was not spent in proposing toasts, and drinking one another's health. No doubt Levi told the company how he was saved, and Jesus would give that *follow* invitation to them all.

And now enter the critics (16), and some good men among them this time (18). These '*were keeping a fast*' while the others *were holding a feast*; and Jesus was with the latter. Some people seem to think that they can find Christ only at funerals! Not so: he performed his first miracle at a wedding. Life for most of us is a strange assortment of fasts and feasts.

Study very carefully verses 21, 22. A new garment does not need a patch and new wineskins will carry any wine.

Also, study carefully verses 27, 28 in their context. This does not mean that you can spend Sunday as you like. If the '*Lord of the sabbath*' is your Lord, you will not be in doubt as to how best to use his day.

Thought: The banquet is spread: sit down.

Christ's cures and curates

Verses 1-6 belong to the picture of *the morning*, which extends from chapter 2:1. This is a picture of *opposition after acclamation*: opposition which is made evident by the way in which certain people related themselves to all that Jesus did. Did he heal and save a sorely stricken man? They said, '*Why?*' and '*Who?*' (2:7). Did he eat with sinners, eager and needy? They still ask, '*Why?*' (2:18). Did his disciples pluck a handful or two of corn as they passed through a field? Again they ask, '*Why?*' (2:24). And now they '*closely watch him*' to see if he would help another needy man on the Sabbath day (2).

These people lived by rule, not by principle; by rote, not by reason; and they have a large posterity. Observe how here Jesus goes to the root of things (4). Everybody is doing either *good* or *evil*, and behind the deed, in the ultimate analysis, is the will to *save* or to *kill*. Stand in the line of this searchlight for a little, and then frankly place yourself. Have *you* a withered hand, doing nothing for Christ?

And now, the third picture — **forenoon or separation** (3:7 to 6:13). '*Jesus withdrew himself with his disciples.*' Sometimes we have to do less in order to do more; to circumscribe our field of action in order to enlarge it. Jesus went away from the throng in order to give more time and attention to a few chosen men, knowing full well that in course of time he would, through them, reach the whole world.

The *training of the twelve* formed a very considerable part of the Saviour's ministry. He did not, at this time, wholly withdraw from the people as verses 7-12 show. What a school these twelve apostles formed; what a conjunction of temperaments and tempers! Who but Jesus could have got the best out of such a scratch team? Remember what they became and accomplished. The master will not *send forth* those who have not first been *with him* (14). If you would instruct, proclaim and expel (15), you must graduate in this school.

Thought: Concentration is strength.

Friend and foes

'*He is out of his mind*' (21). It was not Jesus' avowed enemies who said that, but his kinsmen, his own family (32). The contempt of a foe is hard to bear, but the misunderstanding of a friend is harder. Jesus' family were not ill-disposed towards him; they simply did not understand.

How often men and women who have been *all out* for God have been called mad! People may get as excited as they like about something or nothing, sport, fashion, social events, motor cars, anything, but *they* are not mad; but let someone get enthusiastic about God's love, and enterprising in soul-saving, and he is '*out of his mind*'. Such is the verdict not of foes only, but also of friends. Well, be it so, these Christian fanatics will do more for the world *out of their minds* than any others will do *in their minds*.

But Jesus' enemies went further, and said that he wrought his miracles by Beelzebub. In answer to this charge he says two things: one by way of interrogation; the other by way of affirmation.

'*How can Satan expel Satan?*' Where there is civil war a kingdom cannot last; when a family is split into parties it cannot continue; and in like manner, when Satan makes war upon himself his end is in sight. The charge is absurd.

And secondly, people who think as these scribes did are '*guilty of an eternal sin*' because they say that Christ is devil-possessed (29, 30). Such critics are beyond the reach of further appeal; no moral discernment is left. They say, with Milton's Satan, 'All good to me is lost; evil be thou my good.' 'Can any one now-a-days commit the unpardonable sin?' you ask. This I would say; anyone who is afraid that he has committed it may be quite sure that he has not, for he who has done so has no such fear.

In verses 33-35 Jesus enunciates the new law of relationship with himself. Obedience is the bond.

Thought: Though he is often misunderstood, he never misunderstands.

Soils and souls

It is both interesting and impressive to observe that all Jesus' illustrations were taken from nature and from life. He never, like Paul, employs athletics, for instance, to illustrate any truth; the Creator uses creation for instruction. That is one fact. A second is this, that all his illustrations are amazingly appropriate and simple. In this Gospel we have already had *the old garment and new patch*, and *the new wine and old wineskins*; and now we have the parable of *the soils*. The sower is one, and the seed is one, but there are four kinds of soil.

Christ was a careful observer. It is strange that, although a carpenter by trade, he never draws on that craft for illustration, unless, perhaps, where he says that his *yoke* is easy and light, or, that he is the *door*; but he does say how sowers sow, and how fishermen should fish. Here he compares a *word* to a *seed*, and there are certain analogies which make the one an excellent type of the other.

Both are alive. Seeds are, of course, and so are words. Someone has said they have hands and feet, that they have blood in them; and this is eminently true of the Word of God.

Then, *both have immense reproductive power*. The orchard is in the apple, which is more wonderful than that the apple is in the orchard; and the harvest is in the seed, which is more wonderful than that the seed is in the harvest.

Then, *both the seed and the word must be sown before they can be fruitful*. The seed in the granary will rot, and the word unspoken, or unwritten is barren.

And further, *both are dependent on soil conditions*. Good words may fall into bad minds, as good seed may fall into bad soil. Both the grain and the gospel need congenial surroundings if they are to be fruitful. In some soils neither is productive, and, even in good ground neither is uniformly productive; *'some thirty, some sixty, some an hundred'*. Do you understand?

Thought: The seed tests the soil.

93

Privilege and responsibility

Whatever you call this parable, *the sower, the seed,* or *the soils,* it is the key parable (13), and we should therefore study it with great care.

There are **four kinds of hearers** (14-20). The first class is *insensible*; the gospel takes no hold of them. The second class is *superficial*; the gospel takes only a *temporary hold* of them. The third class is *half-hearted*; the gospel takes a *disputed hold* of them.

Many are the causes of insensibility; by many means the heart may be beaten hard, but chiefly, perhaps, for want of the gospel, or by means of it.

Solemn also is the case of Mr. Temporary, first cousin to Mr. Turn-Back. Fruitage is always a matter of rootage, but this man bears no fruit because his mind and will have never been changed.

Though the third case gives more promise, it is scarcely less sad. In matters spiritual, divided interest and affection are fatal. Here are two crops struggling for the mastery, and there is not nutriment enough for both. Remember that the bearing capacities of the soul are limited.

The good soil, or true soul, has none of these defects. Here are attraction, appropriation and absorption: the seed goes in, gets down, and comes up.

The next is a lesson on **getting and giving** (21-25). Privilege carries with it responsibility; they who have received are under an obligation to impart. Light is for illumination, and they who have it must share it, and they who share it will shine.

The third lesson is on **the promise of productiveness** (26-29). There is here a threefold emphasis. First, *the secret working of truth in the soul* (27); second, *the orderly development of the kingdom of God* (28b); and third, *the fruit-bearing power of the renewed heart* (28a). Meditate prayerfully on each of these, and, encouraged, go back to your work.

Thought: Grow and glow.

The tree and the sea

Our Lord would provoke thought in his disciples by asking: *'Whereunto shall we liken the kingdom of God? Or with what comparison shall we compare it?'* Then he would pause until their imaginations began to glow. They would think of the kingdom as it is depicted in the impassioned pages of the prophets, as great and glorious from the beginning. Imagine now their astonishment when the Master said, *'It is like a grain of mustard seed.'*

Every parable has one main lesson to teach; and the lesson here is derived from comparing *the smallness of the seed when it was sown*, with *the greatness of the tree when it was grown*. Humble beginnings often have exalted issues. Judged by ordinary standards, what could be more insignificant than the career of Jesus himself? On the one hand, think of the lowly birth, the humble home, the carpenter's shop and the cruel cross; and, on the other hand, think of the holy Scriptures, the universal church, the throne of grace, and the coming consummation!

Think of the small beginnings of missionary effort. Look, for instance, at young Carey the cobbler, and then behold the Serampore Institutions, and modern missions of which he was the father. Almost two hundred years ago the heart of John Wesley was 'strangely warmed' in a little meeting house in London. From that sprang the evangelical revival and the Methodist church of today.

Do not despise the day of small things. Think not only of *when it is sown* but also of *when it is grown*.

Jesus now exchanges the shore for the sea, and shows that he is master of raging wind and angry wave. The mighty worker became weary and fell asleep—we all need rest at times—but his weariness was not impotence. *'Have you still no faith?'* (40).

Thought: Encouragement should beget courage.

A cure and the consequences

We see that what proves a blessing to one may easily prove a curse to another. By the coming of Jesus 'into the country of the Gadarenes' *one man was made better, and many were made worse.* The difference is not in the Saviour, but in the attitude of the sinner to him.

There have not been wanting critics who have poured contempt upon this story of the demoniac. Huxley spoke of it as 'the Gadarene pig affair'. Well, Huxley has passed but the story remains. The narrative was not written to tell us that so many pigs were lost, but to tell us of a man who was saved, body and soul. What a hideous ruin of a man is here presented, and it would appear, his state was directly due to his sin! Sin is the great wrecker, and only Christ can salve its wrecks. This man could not help himself, and no one else could do anything for him, but what all the chains of Gadara could not effect, Jesus accomplished by a word.

He did not begin by clothing him, but by saving him. The quickest way to get a man out of the slum is to get the slum out of the man. Social reform is all very well, but the hope of this world is not to be looked for in changed circumstances but in changed hearts.

Alas, that there are those in this story who prefer Christ's room to his company! They who today say to Christ, 'Depart,' will one day hear him say to them, 'Depart.' Are you putting your business before your spiritual welfare? It is a solemn thing to tell Christ to go: sometimes he does, and then what?

Sometimes he tells us to go—not *from* him, however, but *for* him (19). It is often easier to stay than to go, but it is often noblest to do the hardest things. When the once-wicked bear witness to the mighty worker, the people will begin to wonder (20). There is nothing so powerful as personal testimony.

Thought: Oh! The joy of knowing Jesus!
It is dawning on my soul.

Wayside kindness

This is a record of need: the need of a little girl, a Jewish official, and a Gentile woman. Beneath all distinctions of sex and age, of colour and caste, of nationality and office, we all are one in need: when we get down to sorrow and suffering, we get down to bed-rock. This accounts for the fact that it is the sympathisers and not the critics who most are sought, and do most good in the world.

Jairus was greatly concerned about the welfare of his daughter. What about yours? Moral and spiritual sickness is infinitely worse than any physical ailment. Some sinners would be better dead than living as they are. Well, Jesus went with Jairus. He was never too busy to do good, because he was always busy doing good.

On the way to the house he was held up. That must greatly have tried the patience of the ruler, yet we are not told that he complained. A poor Gentile woman, suffering from haemorrhage, who, without deriving any benefit, had put her limited savings into the pockets of the doctors, came in her extremity to Jesus. Her faith was small, but it was faith, and Jesus acknowledged it (34). She had but one opportunity, and she seized it, and greatly was she blessed.

But blessing is costly, that is, to the blesser. When this woman touched Jesus' garment, healing power *went forth from him*. Do we try to do good easily and cheaply? Such good is scarcely worth doing. Healing goodness always costs. Many *thronged* Christ at this time, but only one *touched* him.

Saving blessing is never accidental but always deliberate; *my faith must connect with his power*. No one will slip into heaven in a crowd. The crowd is not going that way; and though it did, the gate is narrow. Can you name two greater blessings than these — *health* (whole), and *peace* (34)?

Thought: Do all the good you can as you go.

The discipline of delay

I have said that the delay of Jesus caused by the action of this woman must have been a great trial to Jairus; but what can his emotions have been when the word came, '*Your daughter is dead*'? In similar circumstances how would you feel? Surely the countenance of the ruler at that moment must have revealed a broken heart, for he seems never to have thought that the power of Christ reached not only up to death, but beyond it.

Truly the delays of Christ are oft times very perplexing. Martha and Mary thought so, as well as Jairus. '*If thou hadst been here, my brother had not died.*' Then, why was he not there? Because he knows, as we never can, what power he has, and when he restrains it, we may be sure it is for our larger good. His delays are not denials, but they are discipline.

When Jesus arrived, the professional mourners were already in the house, making the place ring with their shrill lamentations. From the room where the corpse lay, these were summarily dismissed, and but five persons were allowed to enter. When Jesus said that the little girl was only sleeping, he was not denying that life was extinct, but he was giving his view of death. On another occasion, he said, 'Our friend Lazarus sleepeth; but I go, that I may awake him out of sleep.' The only death that Jesus knew, and that the Christian should know, is that which is 'the wages of sin'. Of departed saints it is said that they '*sleep in Jesus*' (1 Thessalonians 4:14). And so the passing of this child was *a sleep*, and Jesus wakened her.

I wonder if she ever said anything about where she had been? Why does the story end here? What did Jairus say? And what did he do? I wonder! Enough has been told us to show that he who could staunch the flow of blood could also break the bands of death. He is Lord in every realm!

Thought: God works for them who wait for him.

At home and abroad

Today's portion is wonderfully full of lessons, and all I can hope to do within our limits is to gather up a little of this dust of gold. There are two main passages—*Jesus at home* and *the apostles abroad.*

● **Jesus at home** (1-6). Two facts are made clear in this record: the fact that *Jesus was human* (3), and the fact that *he was divine* (2). He was like, and yet unlike others. He was so humanly normal that his folks at home did not know that he was the fulfilment of all prophecy and the hope of all ages. They observed that his *words* and *wisdom* and *works* were distinctive (2), but instead of studying him, '*they were scandalised in him*' (3). Obviously Jesus was not the mere product of his race, and he owed little to heredity or environment. It may be difficult to believe that he was God, but is it not more difficult to believe that he is not?

Unbelief paralyses power (5a): where moral conditions are wanting, omnipotence is impotent. Yet there is no such thing as total failure where Christ is. '*He laid his hands upon a few sick folk, and healed them*' (5). This should cheer many a discouraged worker. Does Christ *wonder* at your unbelief (6)?

● **The apostles abroad** (7-13). Now he turns from the city to the villages (6), where he won most of his triumphs. Evangelise the villages: India and China are worlds of villages. But before you go, come; the school first, then the field; in order to teach we must learn, and we learn in order to teach.

This beginning of the missionary enterprise was very small: only six couples of preachers; but see whereunto it has grown! Among the hills near Moffat in Scotland is a small board on a pole, bearing these words, 'Source of river Tweed'. At Berwick you may see the river merging into the sea. The greatest issues have had humble origins; trickles in the mountains become torrents in the valleys. These twelve provincials have become the church of God. Therefore, '*care not*', and '*fear not*'.

Thought: The oak is in the acorn.

Three men and two women

Chronologically, verses 17-29 precede verses 14-16; let us therefore, look first of all at **Herod and John** (17-29). The story of the one is as dark as that of the other is bright. What a contrast! Palace and desert, luxury and poverty, society and loneliness, moral weakness and moral strength, cowardice and courage, fear and faith, iniquity and righteousness, apparent success which was failure, and apparent failure which was success. Herod carries the brand of shame, but John wears the hero's crown.

Death is sometimes more glorious than life; certainly John's death was better than Herod's life. Herod attained to notoriety, but John to fame; mark the difference. It is sometimes safer to be silent than to speak, but loyalty is better than safety. What applies to motoring is not good advice for morals: 'Safety first'. John had more respect for his conscience than for his head, and lost the latter to save the former. Herod knew more than he was prepared to live up to (20), and in this he is like many people. It is nothing short of tragedy to have noble ideas and low pursuits, sublime thoughts and degrading habits. Is your life a sublime unity, or a pathetic contradiction?

● **Jesus and Herod** (14-16). Some heads are more powerful on a platter than others on their shoulders. Though John was dead, he was not done with. When Herod heard of Jesus, he thought that John had risen from the dead. 'Conscience doth make cowards of us all.' What a compliment to John to think that Jesus was he! And Jesus did not repudiate the comparison.

Observe that all these verdicts of Jesus are good: *John, Elijah, a prophet*. What or whom do you remind people of? Something or someone good or bad? We know that Christ was better than the best that has ever been.

Thought: Be true to God and your own soul.

Resting by working

What a wonderful story this is! The Master and his disciples seek a retreat; they are followed by hungry and eager crowds; the disciples have their idea of what to do with these people, and Jesus has his, and these ideas do not harmonise. The disciples talk of buying what they have not, but Jesus thinks of blessing what they have.

Like the people, lessons crowd in upon us here.

● **The need of rest** (30-32). Mark the context. These disciples returned to their Master from *service* (30), and with *sorrow* (29), and therefore they needed rest. Made as we are, sorrow brings shock, and shock must not be ignored. We have to face the fact of reactions, physical and mental; not to do so is to court further trouble. Service also is exhausting, and we need time for reflection and renewal. To deny oneself this, is to mortgage the future. Underline these three words: '*apart, rest, leisure*' (31). Are you tired? The time for rest has arrived. Don't live on your capital.

● **The claim of the unexpected** (33-37a). The rest sought was not found, the retreat invaded, the much-needed quiet was not allowed. Most busy workers have had that experience, and what matters at such a time is our attitude to the unexpected.

All had earned rest, and might have insisted on it; but when big claims come suddenly upon us out of the void, we should respond to them in a big way, and look to God to give us the strength we so greatly need. We do not read that the disciples were any the worse for working overtime; were they not infinitely the better? Times come when we have nobly to forget ourselves to serve the need of others, and then even work is rest.

Thought: How satisfying is the food of faith!

Signs on sea and shore

Is Mark's record a fairy story or sober fact? Certainly it is a 'book of wonders'. Here is one who can feed 15,000 — 20,000 people with five loaves and two fishes, who can walk on the stormy sea and who can heal all who will touch him; surely such a one was divine; and yet he was human, for he needed rest (31), and was dependent on prayer (46). This is the ever-challenging mystery-fact, none the less a mystery though a fact, and none the less a fact though a mystery. The Son of God is the son of man.

This mighty worker was the first to begin (1:35), and the last to finish (45). There can be no eight-hour-day in this service. Jesus prayed before he started his day's work, and he prayed again when he had finished it. Do you? The greatest argument for prayer is the fact that Christ prayed.

This sea experience was a strange one for the disciples. What exactly was it designed to teach them, and us? What is its moral value? Maybe we cannot escape the stormy sea, but let us believe that we need not be without the Lord of wind and wave. Does his presence *trouble* you (50)? Have you failed to understand his past dealings with you (52)? Well, he does not come now with words of blame, but of cheer (50), and his presence brings calm (51).

What is made emphatic in verses 53-56 is not the people's *faith*, but their *need*. There is something pathetic in this age-long eagerness to get quit of handicap and to live. The quest is often misdirected, but it is always pursued. The business of the Christian and of the church is to direct this need to the true supply (56).

Thought: Christ is always nearer to us than we suppose.

Commandment versus tradition

We have here a quibble and a lesson. The Pharisees do the quibbling, and Jesus does the teaching. The question is one of *ablutions* and *obligations*: the Pharisees stand for the former, and Jesus for the latter.

Two kinds of defilement are here in view: outer, and inner; defilement of the body and defilement of the soul. Which, think you, is the worse? Both body and soul should be clean. The religion of these people consisted of outward observances, in keeping rules and cleaning surfaces: it therefore was superficial and unreal. What God looks at is the state of our hearts, not the condition of our skin and crockery.

No one can tell what damage has been done to the cause of true religion in the world by just such religiosity as these men exhibited. What they had was neither religion (3,4), nor ethics (10-13), but triviality and trickery. Their worship was vain and in vain, because it was of the lip and not of the heart (6,7).

Have we yet learned that what comes out of our hearts is of more consequence than what goes into our mouths (15,20-23), and that which matters is not our cups but our characters, not our table, but our temper? We are under obligation both to God and one another; to neglect the one is irreligious, and to neglect the other is unethical, and these men did both.

With the pen of your will, write today on the tablet of your heart, with the ink of sincerity: *resolved that now and ever, I will be real, and not a pretender; I will fear and worship God, and do my duty by my fellows.*

Thought: Dwell deep.

Stroke and counterstroke

This story of **the Syrophoenician woman** (25-30), is profoundly interesting. It is one of the numerous passages where Mark's
narrative seems to be the description of an eye-witness. Peter
heard the words and saw the effect on the woman.

Why did she come to Christ? Because she had heard that he
could, and would help those who were in trouble, and she was
in trouble (25). Her little girl had a demon. Then is childhood
exposed to the ravages of wicked spirits? Yes, alas, the devil has
no respect for the simplicity and innocence of little children; he
will take what he can get.

Observe this mother's concern: she *came* and *straightway*
fell down at Jesus' feet and *besought* his help and *pleaded* with
him until she *got* what she wanted.

To test her faith, Jesus raised an objection (27) by reminding
her that she was a Gentile 'dog', softening the expression,
however, by using the diminutive. This, the woman astutely
seized upon, and claimed for herself the crumbs to which 'little
household dogs' were entitled (28). As Luther has said, 'She
snares Christ in his own words,' and immediately obtains the
blessing sought. Her Abrahamic faith is rewarded.

Christ's attention is now turned to the case of **a man who
was deaf and dumb** (32-37). Mark, only, records this. No case
was ever brought to Jesus that beat him, as we say, and your
case is not likely to be the first. Deaf, or dumb, or blind, or
palsied, or demon-possessed, or dead, Christ can give you what
you need: hearing, or speech, or sight, or health, or freedom,
or life. His methods vary, but his purpose never. *'He hath done
all things well.'*

Thought: We cannot tell until we hear.

The hungry are fed

Twice Jesus fed a crowd, and both times in similar circumstances and in the same way. Comparing the two narratives, there are the hungry folk, the desert place, the perplexed disciples, the meagre provisions, the command to be seated, the thanksgiving, the feast, the surplus and the dismissal. And contrasting them there are: one day and three days; 5,000 and 4,000; five loaves and two fishes and seven loaves and a few fishes; twelve baskets and seven baskets. Nor were these baskets the same. In chapter 6, they were wicker baskets, but here they are large hand-baskets, like the one by which Paul was let down over the wall of Damascus. In verses 19,20 Jesus uses two different words (Gr.) for '*baskets*'. The first feast is recorded by all four evangelists; this one, by Matthew and Mark only.

How little progress the apostles made in understanding! 'The mighty interpositions of God's hand in former passages of men's lives fall out of their memories. Each new difficulty appears insurmountable, as one from which there is no extraction; at each recurring necessity it seems as though the wonders of God's grace are exhausted, and had come to an end' (Trench). Are we slow like that, or does our past experience of God help us to face each new situation with courage and confidence?

I cannot but believe that Christ saw in these two feeding miracles what no one else present saw; a figure of his own coming passion. He was the bread broken to satisfy the hunger of the world. Have you partaken of the feast?

Why did Jesus *sigh* (12)? Was it not because here he was being tempted to do what the devil had tried to get him to do in the great temptation — openly declare his Messiahship? He knew that by refusing to give the signs asked for, he would be rejected by the leaders of the nation.

Thought: Do what you believe to be right, whatever the consequences.

Two kinds of blindness

The Master is hurt. Why? Because he was misunderstood by those who should have known him best. That always hurts, and there are many who, this very day, are feeling it keenly.

How did the disciples misunderstand Jesus? In two ways. First, they thought that he was speaking about literal leaven; and second, they thought that he was blaming them for having forgotten to take into the boat a sufficient supply of bread. Of course, Jesus was doing neither, and he wondered that they had not understood him.

Observe that in this brief conversation he asks nine questions, and some of them are haunting. *'Do ye not remember?'* *'Do ye not yet understand?'* Is not Christ still asking these questions of you and me? He means us to profit in the present from lessons in the past, but do we (19,20)?

When he spoke of *leaven* he referred to evil, and to three manifestations of it: the *hypocrisy* of the Pharisees, the *worldliness* of the Herodians, and the *unbelief* of the Sadducees (Matthew 16:6). These, not infrequently, are allied to strict religious observances; they were in that day; they are in this.

Now, what is the use of eyes and ears if we do not see and hear? What is the use of faculties which do not function? By *hardened heart* Christ means, not a callous, but a dull, not-understanding heart; and, remember, he is speaking to *disciples*.

The incident of the blind man of Bethsaida Julius (22-26) is related by Mark only. Observe that the miracle was gradual, and that external signs were employed. Read verses 24, 25 in the RV. The state of this man when he saw dimly (24) we may liken to one who is converted, but not dedicated; to one who sees, but not clearly. Have you received the *second touch* (25)?: not till then will you be able to look *steadfastly*. Our souls need the *oil* as well as the *blood*.

Thought: Light is for sight.

File leader and follower

This is a great and solemn portion. Compare verse 28 with 6:14,15, and observe again that all these estimates of Jesus are good. He reminded the people of some great man of the past. Of whom do we remind people? Observe, *men* and *ye* in verses 27,29: people in general, and his own disciples. If I asked you who men were saying I was, or what you yourself thought of me, would you not conclude that I was suffering from the disease of self-importance? But this is not true of Christ. He had a divine self-consciousness, and so a sense of authority and power, and of having been sent into this world on an unique mission. We should never fail to weigh the significance, not only of Christ's claims for himself, but also of the verdicts of others concerning him, which he accepted. He was not horrified when Peter said he was *the Christ,* as you and I would be if that were said of us: he accepted it, and so endorsed it.

But he would not have them or us mistake the nature of his mission, or the manner of its fulfilment. His victory could be only by seeming defeat; the crown could be reached only by the cross (31). Peter, at any rate, did not understand that (32), and so the rebuker was rebuked (33).

And now follows one of the profoundest of all the Master's utterances (34-38). *Self-denial, cross-bearing, and discipleship all go together, and no one can lay claim to the latter, of whom the former are not true* (34). In the matter of *life* we lose by saving, and save by losing; we die by living, and live by dying (35). This is a truth which the world cannot understand, and which it is to be feared, the church does not practise.

The whole world when put in the scale with the *soul* is feather-light; these were never of commensurate value; and when once a soul is *lost,* there is nothing in the universe which can be offered in exchange for it (36,37). *There is no compensation for the loss of the soul, in either time or eternity.*

Thought: Live for his smile at last.

On and from the mountain-top

I take the Transfiguration to be the fulfilment of verse 1, and the three disciples (2) to be the *'some of them that stand here'*. What else could it mean? Points to be considered here are the setting, place, time, occasion, purpose, details, and effect of the Transfiguration. Contemplate the glorified Christ, the assembled persons, and the heavenly witness. Christ is central, as he ever must be.

Of the five accompanying persons, two represent the Old Testament—Moses, standing for law, and Elijah for prophecy; and three represent the New Testament—Peter, James and John. Together they represent the bride of the Lamb, by which is meant (I submit) neither Israel nor the church, but all in every dispensation who have a saving interest in the Lamb.

The representatives of the two great covenants gather round Christ, and acknowledge by their presence, that he is the goal of the one, and the starting-point of the other; that in him all the hope of mankind focuses.

But after the mountain, the valley; after the heights, the hollows; after the glory, the gloom; after the rapture, the rebuke. Experience is kaleidoscopic. But this does not mean that the purpose of God is that we should live an up-and-down life all the time. Rather, his will is that we should bring the glory of the height into the gloom of the valley, and by the inspiration of the mountain prepare for the obligation of the plain. There is a sense in which we can, and a sense in which we cannot, always dwell on the sunlit peaks.

How patient Jesus was with these dull disciples (9-13). How little they understood, but at least they were willing to learn. I would rather be dull and eager, than clever and indolent. Elijah is historic, intermediate, and prophetic. The first and third are the same person, the Tishbite; the second is John the Baptist. 'Understandest thou what thou readest?'

Thought: Store sunshine for wintry days.

Faltering faith

Over against the impotence of these disciples we have Christ's power; over against this father's distress, Christ's compassion; and over against the people's perplexity, Christ's enlightenment.

How pathetic is the case of these eight disciples! They had had power conferred on them to exorcise evil spirits, yet now they were unable to do so. Why? They were depressed. A week before (2) their Master had given them the staggering news of his approaching death (8:31), and they had not recovered from the shock; and moreover, he and the three chief disciples were absent when this claim came upon them (18). Furthermore, their spiritual vitality had been lowered by lack of prayer (29). These things together are more than enough to account for their failure.

Do you never get depressed? Do you never fail? We all do, and there is always a reason, and generally it is not far to seek. But now, as then, Christ always appears at the time of need (14,15).

But not on account of these failing followers is this son to go unhealed, nor his father unblessed. The latter's faith had been shaken and must now be restored. How pathetic is his appeal: *'If thou canst do anything, have compassion on us and help us.'* By *us* the father means that he suffers in his boy's sufferings and healing of him will bring relief to his father-heart. That is *sympathy*. Jesus repeats the father's words, *'if thou canst!'* (see RV).

Do you believe that *'all things are possible to him that believeth'*? It is not a question of Christ's ability to impart, but of our ability to receive; not of his *power* but of our *faith*. Christ will help us *if* we apply to him. Study carefully this father's prayer (24). Both belief and unbelief are here, but he wants more of the one, and none of the other. Do you?

After this, Jesus again foretells his death (see verse 12 and 8:31).

Thought: Demons fly when faith functions.

Life lessons which should be learnt

Several lessons cluster here.

● **Humility** (33-37). Here, after the glory of the Mount, after the shame of failure, after the story of coming suffering, these disciples are arguing with one another as to which of them was the greater. Before we blame them, let us examine ourselves. Of course they are blameworthy; they were dunces in Christ's school, and though men, they acted like boys, and wanted to 'show off'. Christ taught them, and teaches us, that the servant is chief, the last is first, the humblest is greatest. When shall we believe that truly enough to live by it?

● **Tolerance** (38-41). Read again the story and then concentrate on the great lesson; *'He that is not against us is for us'*. With this compare Matthew 12:33! These utterances are not contradictory but supplementary. May it not be said that the latter refers to one's relation to Christ himself and the former to one's relation to other disciples? If one is not *with Christ*, of course one is *against him*; but it does not follow, if that one is not *with us* that therefore he is *against us*. We cannot claim, as Christ could, to be the norm of truth, the test of reality. He that is not *with us* may be nearer to Christ than we are.

● **Offences** (42-48). Offences first against others (41,42) and then against ourselves (43-48). We have no right to make it more difficult for other people to live, and he had better not have lived who has made life insufferable for others. But neither have we any right to impair our own life, and rather than do so, we should fearlessly practice spiritual surgery. It is the free, full life that is forceful; a saltless life is a silly life, seek pungency and peace (49,50).

Thought: The problem of life is one of true adjustments.

The subjects of the kingdom

Collect and classify all passages which record Jesus' teaching on *marriage and divorce*, and those also which refer to Jesus and *children*, and mark carefully what they teach. Here, for instance (10:1-12—on marriage and divorce, and 9:33-37, 42; 10:13-16—on children).

In what sense does the kingdom of God belong to children and how does a little child receive the kingdom of God? A little child in Jesus' arms—how profoundly significant! Nothing is more important than study of, and service for, the children.

Now surely it is the privilege and duty of all parents to bring their children to Christ, even as these did (13). Sometimes it is the child who brings the parent. The child need not become a man before he comes to Christ, but the man must become a child if he would come (15).

But from the child we pass to *the man* (17-22). It is a simple, sad story. Here is one who really wanted something more and better than he had, but he was not prepared to make any sacrifices to get it. If Christ could agree to such a thing, millions of people would join the church at once. But *no*: law-keeping is no more Christianity than money-loving; this man did both, but missed what mattered.

You say, he lacked only *one thing*! Yes, but what a thing! A watch may lack only a main spring; a motor may lack only an engine; a dial may lack only an iron finger: but of what use are watch and car and dial? The *one thing* which this man lacked was the thing that mattered first and last, for time and eternity. Having silver was no compensation for the want of salvation. What is the good of gold if you miss God? Christ does not teach that one who has money cannot enter into the kingdom of God (23-27), but that if gold, or anything else, is a hindrance, it must be put aside. Regeneration is better than riches, but if you have both, the one should teach you how to use the other.

Thought: Christ is our wealth.

The question of rewards

Do you do what you do for what you can get, or because it is the right thing to do (28)? It would not be right to say that the hope of reward should never be a motive for sacrifice, but such a motive needs constant cleansing, for it can easily become defiled. But Christ here teaches that no sacrifice for him goes unrewarded, either here or hereafter.

There is *a hundredfold now in this time*. Is that true? It does not mean, of course, that he who sacrifices a house will get a hundred houses, but it does mean that there will come to him who yields all to Christ, a present enlargement and enrichment of life beyond all imagination, as well as perfection and glory at last. And Christ teaches also, that part of that enrichment comes by means of *persecutors*; not in spite of them, but by means of them (30). Welcome the tools which are giving you eternal shape.

As Jesus drew nearer to the cross, he became more explicit in what he said to his disciples about it. They should have understood, but evidently they did not. Why did Jesus speak about this so often? Of course it was in order to prepare these men for that event; but was it not also because his own heart craved for sympathy? And he did not get it. Is he today craving for something from you to which he has every right, but is not getting it? How little the disciples understood is seen in the next paragraph (35-40).

Why should James and John want the best seats? Why should you or I? We all shall get at last what we shall have let him make us worthy to receive. Our place in heaven will not be determined by greed, but by grace. Let us be more concerned about our sanctification on earth than our seat in glory.

Thought: The humble shall be exalted.

Teacher and healer

Why were the ten indignant at the request of the two? Because they also wanted place and power; they were all ambitious in a wrong way. The situation is serious; there is schism in this circle; what is to be done? *'Jesus called them to him.'* When Christian folk get cross with one another the best thing is to get together, on the understanding always that it is Christ who is calling them, and that he will preside. With what amazing patience and tact he handles this situation!

He sets before these disciples two examples: the world's and his own; and this amounts to saying, 'Now which of these will you follow?' In the world it is the king who is great, but in the kingdom, it is the servant. Brass buttons and an officious bearing do not contribute greatness, but living for others does.

The standards of the world and the kingdom are a universe apart. If we want worldly greatness, we shall adopt wordly ideals and pursue worldly methods; but if we want heavenly greatness, we must understand that we can attain thereunto, not by self-importance, but by self-sacrifice. Of this, Christ himself is the greatest example (45).

As for Bartimaeus, surely he is a standing rebuke to multitudes. There was something which he desperately needed; he knew this, and was determined to get it; and wherever these three things are found together, something will happen. The crowd did their best to keep this man and Jesus apart, but though his sight was defective, his lungs were not, and he used them to good purpose. *'What wilt thou that I should do unto thee?'* With Christ is conscious power; is there with you conscious need? God is now willing; are you? *'Believe ye that I am able to do this?'* Bartimaeus said, *'Rabboni'*—my dear Master. So did Mary, on the resurrection morning. Have you ever said that?

Thought: Follow him in the way.

Sunday and Monday

The proclamation and the coronation of a king never go together. This is Christ's proclamation (1-10); his first coronation came later on in that same week; his second is going on all the time in loyal hearts; and his third will be when he comes again to establish his kingdom.

The king has many subjects, but all are not true. The unknown disciple (1-6), represents the one class, and the shouting crowd (7-10), represents the other. It is always easier to shout than to obey. Which are you doing?

Observe where this triumphal entry of the king ended. Not in Caesar's palace, but in the Temple (11), because his kingdom is spiritual and not temporal.

Observe also what he did this Sunday morning in the Temple (11). *'He looked round about upon all things.'* That is what he does every Sunday morning, in your church, and in mine. I wonder what he sees! Certainly everything that is there. His last Sunday evening before Calvary he spent at Bethany with those who loved him best (11).

On Monday, he was early on the road, going towards Jerusalem (12-14). Why was he hungry at such an hour? Presumably he had had no breakfast. But why? In all likelihood he had slipped out of the home 'a great while before day' and had spent some hours in prayer on Olivet. His Father's fellowship was more to him than his necessary food.

The cursing of the fig-tree was an acted parable. The tree represents Israel; the leaves, their religious profession; the want of fruit, their spiritual barrenness; *'seen afar off '*, their conspicuous position; the Lord's approach, the Messiah's claim; and the curse, the rejection of that generation.

Christ cleansed the Temple twice, at the beginning, and at the end of his ministry (15-18). Whom would he have to clear out if he came to your church in actual person?

Thought: Your heart is the throne he wants.

Tuesday

What a Tuesday that was in Passion Week! Was there ever a busier day, even in the life of the Great Worker? Its happenings carry us from 11:20 to 14:11. Make a note of that, please, in the margin of your Bible. I suppose you recognise the difference between *power* and *authority*. In the New Testament the word for the one is *dunamis* and for the other, *exousia*. Verses 20-26 are about the former, and verses 27-33 are about the latter.

● **Prayer power** (20-26). Christ's answer to Peter's question is not what he or we expected, and indeed, the answer seems irrelevant, yet it cannot be in reality. Is it not as though Jesus said, 'If one is living in touch with God, what he does will be right, and he will be irresistible'? Faith is more dynamic than gun-cotton, if only for the reason that it operates in more than one world. Before the faith of the early church, the mountain of Judaism was uprooted, and another mountain planted in its place. The history of Christian missions is one long illustration of what Christ here declares.

Observe that *faith* does not wait to *feel*. 'All things whatsoever ye pray and ask for, believe that ye have *received* (Greek) them, and ye shall have them' (24, RV). *So faith takes before it gets.*

● **Divine authority** (27-33). Here again Jesus' reply appears to be irrelevant, but it is not. What had *the baptism of John* to do with *the authority of Jesus*? The missions of these two were intimately related, and must stand or fall together. John said that Jesus was the Messiah. If John was right, then there was no need to ask Jesus by what authority he wrought. Christ's reply was a masterpiece of dialectic. They who do not acknowledge his *authority* can never exercise prayer *power*; we can accomplish only as we obey.

Thought: Ask and believe.

The fate of the faithless

The key to this parable is in verse 12: 'They (11:27, RV) *perceived that he spake the parable against them.*' Read it in the light of their consciousness, and it will be a mirror in which is reflected a large part of their national history.

In the *planting* we see their origin, the *hedge* tells of protection, the *pit* of provision, the *tower* of precaution, and the *husbandman* of purpose. The *man who planted* represents Jehovah, and the *servants* are the prophets, the *husbandmen* being the religious leaders of the people. The *son* is, of course, Jesus Christ. Is not this a striking and solemn picture of the Jewish nation at that time! This people likened here to the vine, in 11:12-14 to the fig-tree, and in Romans 11:17 to the olive tree. The vine represents their past, the fig their present, and the olive their future.

With today's passage read Isaiah 5:1-7. The history of Israel, as here set forth, is one of opportunities neglected, privileges abused, and trust betrayed. Let us remember that responsibility is always in the measure of privilege, and that we have no right to presume upon the divine patience.

Where there is faithlessness, sooner or later there will be deprivation. Christ has a right to expect fruit from you and me, and if instead of yielding it, we resist, as an interference, his approaches to his own property, then what but judgement can we expect?

Study carefully verse 6. It is 'of immense significance for the self-consciousness of Jesus'. Observe, he represents himself as the only and beloved Son of the owner of the vineyard, one to whom reverence is due. Could any mere man speak of himself in this way? This claim of Christ for himself is either true, or not true.

Thought: Be true to your trust.

Talk traps

Tricks and traps in the matter of talk are as foolish as they are dangerous. A person has only to be a clever dialectician, and he can make the crooked look straight, and the wrong appear to be right. There are two things we should all cultivate: clear thinking, and plain speaking; mean what you say, and say what you mean.

That is what these Pharisees did not do (13-15a). Their estimate of Christ was truer than they imagined, or intended. Every straight-thinking man or woman will put *the way of God* before the *person of men;* but the rarest thing in the world is to find a straight-thinking person. Christ is the divine wisdom; all his teaching illustrates this. No wonder these men marvelled at this answer (15b-17). Let us learn from it that we have civic as well as religious duties; there is Caesar as well as God.

The next assailants were the Sadducees (18-23). Their question was speculative, not practical and political like the former. They tell of a woman who had seven husbands, and then, not without a touch of humour, they say, *'Last of all the woman died also.'* Then they wonder how these seven men are going to settle the problem of possession in the next life. Of course, the Sadducees did not believe in a next life, so that if it was seven of them the woman had married, they were quite safe, according to their view.

In his reply (24-27) Jesus teaches great truths: that there is another life; that there is to be a resurrection of the body; that the social relations of earth do not persist in the next world; that there are such beings as angels; that they do not live socially as we do; and that Abraham, Isaac and Jacob are alive now. These Sadducees were ignorant alike of divine truth and power (24). Why should we be so eager to advertise our ignorance?

Thought: Words are creatures with hands and feet.

The insight of Jesus

Among all these quibblers is one genuine questioner; among all these word-trappers is one hunter of knowledge: *'What commandment is the first of all?'* He asked for the first, and Jesus gave him the first and second. Both are based upon the being, unity and sovereignty of God: *'the Lord our God is one Lord'* (Deuteronomy 6:4). That is the first creed and the foundation of every true creed.

Let any part of this be denied or disproved, and no need or use remains of considering anything else. But that great fact granted, other great truths necessarily follow; the most important being that we, who are God's creatures, should love him, and love one another, and *do* so unreservedly, from and with *all* our heart, soul, mind and strength. There cannot be neighbour-love where there is not self-love (31). In what sense should we love ourselves?

This scribe accepted the verdict of his teacher, and the teacher vouchsafed a verdict on this man: *'Thou art not far from the kingdom of God.'* Then, he hadn't arrived; so near, and yet not within! Is that your case? Remember, you may graze the very gates of heaven on the way to hell.

In verses 35-37 two things are declared: that David's Son is his Lord, that is, that Christ is divine; and that David himself believed this when he wrote Psalm 110, the critics notwithstanding.

In verses 38-40 hypocrites and humbugs are expected, and their doom declared. Why should you wish to appear to be what really in your heart you despise? Our highest place is lying low at our Redeemer's feet.

In verses 41-44 we have Christ's verdict on the collection. It is still true that the 'multitude cast *brass* (Greek) into the treasury' (41); and it is still true that it is sacrificial giving which is most acceptable to God. He sees what you give.

Thought: Where are you in relation to the kingdom?

Christ predicts

This is a wonderful chapter, and the parallel accounts should be read for other details: Matthew 24,25; Luke 21. The nation had rejected their Messiah, and now he rejects them, and foretells the doom of their capital, and their own sufferings.

Verses 1,2, are plain enough, but 3,4, are not so easy to understand. These disciples asked, *when?* and *what?* Should they not have asked *why?* and *how?* It would have revealed in them a deeper concern for their own nation if, instead of being curious about *time* and *signs*, they had inquired what was the *cause* of so stern a judgement, and by what *means* it might yet be averted. Abram did better for Sodom long before, than these men do for Jerusalem now. Are you in the grip of curiosity or concern?

In reading this chapter, it is all important that we get the right perspective, and to do this we must use binoculars for the sake of focus. Two judgements are here in view, a *near* and a *far*. The one refers to the destruction of Jerusalem, forty years later, AD 70; and the other, to the end of the present age. These two are clearly distinguished in Luke's account, the AD 70 event being given in 21:12-24 (mark the words, *'but before all these'* (12), and *'until'* (24), and the end-of-the-age event in 21:5-11, 25-36). This distinction is most important.

Well, how does Jesus reply to the curiosity of his disciples as to time and signs? He says, *'Take heed that no man lead you astray'* (5, RV). Many good people take more heed to the future than to the present, and seem to be more interested in coming events than in Christian character. It is quite certain that Christ will come again, but the best proof we can give that we believe this, is that by steadfastness and diligence we prepare ourselves for that event, should it occur in our time. Observe, Christ never promised his followers that they would have an easy time, but he did and does assure us of *salvation* now and at the end (13). Then 'carry on'.

Thought: The faithful can never fail.

Tribulation trouble

This portion may puzzle many a reader, but observe, it says, *'Let him that readeth understand,'* (14) therefore what is said must be intelligible; what is required is that we be intelligent. *'The abomination of desolation'* sends us to the Old Testament to Daniel 9:27; 11:31; 12:11. From a comparison of these passages with other prophecies, and John's Apocalypse, we shall see that a period of judgement is predicted called *the Tribulation* (19, 24, see Revelation 7:14, RV). Our portion tells of this period in verses 14-23, and of what will happen *'after'* it, in verses 24-27.

The whole utterance is Jewish in complexion of whatever period we interpret it, but that it points to *the end of the age* seems clear from the declaration of verses 26, 27. The history of the Jews is one of suffering, but this must not be regarded as their misfortune, but rather as the discipline rendered necessary by their repeated apostasies. Greatly privileged, they have greatly sinned, and greatly have they suffered, and shall continue so to do until they acknowledge as their Messiah him whom they pierced.

But the judgement here spoken of, will not move within the limits of the Jewish nation; it will affect the whole world. *'Sun, moon and stars'* (24) may be read literally, but it is much more likely that powers and authorities, peoples and individuals are meant.

The last war made it clear that the whole world is involved in the fate of any of its parts, so that no longer can judgement be local. Furthermore, it is certain that the Jews everywhere have longings for a national homeland and these are already taking shape (28). When that day comes, the whole world will be affected thereby. You see then, that such a prophecy as this falls well within the compass of practical politics. History is forewritten.

Thought: Pray for the Jews.

An uncertain certainty

Do what we will, we can never get rid of the predictive element in Scripture without getting rid of Scripture itself, for it is in the very warp and woof of it. This acknowledged, we should remember further, that there is progressive *interpretation* as well as progressive *revelation*. Prophecy forecasts history; history confirms prophecy, and some parts of the Bible will never be properly understood until the day when its prophecy is fulfilled. Yet, it is true that there are *signs* which shall herald the coming of the King. *Our* conceptions of time and space do not apply here; the viewpoint is heaven's. We must so interpret the words, *'nigh'* and *'at the doors'* (29).

The passage before us says three things with utmost plainness: first that Christ is to come again; second that we do not know when he will come; and third, that we should be looking for him all the time. It has been said that those who, in generations gone by, expected Christ to come in their time, were mistaken. That is not so. They were watching without knowing. The spirit of expectation is enjoined, and is true, and in one of these generations he will come. We do not watch because we know, but just because we do not know. If we definitely knew that Christ would not come until a particular date what would be the good of watching between this and then?

A difficulty is cleared away if we assume that by verse 30 is meant the generation *of* which and not *to* which he was speaking. How wonderful that the Lord of glory should consent to accept limitations of knowledge while here on earth (32)! Who is the *porter* of verse 34? What a terrible thing it would be to be *sleeping* when Christ comes (35)! Could we ever forgive ourselves?

Thought: Watch through every watch.

Hate and love

It is still Tuesday of Passion Week but this full and wonderful day is drawing to a close. As to the order of events, it will be well to observe that verses 3-9 are out of their setting. The anointing of Jesus by Mary of Bethany belongs to the close of the Perean ministry, and immediately before the opening of Passion Week, and therefore comes in between chapters ten and eleven of this Gospel. But what a setting is now given to the incident! Here is love in a frame of hate (1,2, 3-9, 10,11). Jesus attracted, and he repelled; he did, and he does; he sends at once peace, and a sword.

We shall not dwell on the hellish plot of the priests and scribes, and the part Judas played in it; but look at Mary and her deed. Simon had been a leper, and most likely this feast was an expression of his gratitude to Jesus for having healed him. The anointing by Mary was also the expression of the love of three hearts for what had been done for them (John 11). Are you grateful for what Christ has done for you? How have you shown it? No one has ever been so generous in appreciation and praise as Christ (6-9); as much for the two mites of the widow, as for Mary's costly nard.

Love is always lavish; it is not cautious but reckless; not niggardly but prodigal in its giving. Poor, shrivelled souls will always say, *'What waste!'* and feign indignation and a care for the poor (4,5). Was it *waste* when Paton went to the New Hebrides? When Morrison went to China, Martyn to India, Mary Slessor to Africa? Was it waste? Many think so, but Christ does not, and that's what matters.

Many lessons are in verses 12-16. Often when Christ's public friends forsake him, his private friends reveal themselves. Perhaps this man (13) was Mark, and this feast held in his house. Can Christ reckon on you in the day of trouble?

Thought: What shall I render unto the Lord?

In the upper room

We cannot but be impressed with the sense of the essential which Mark's brevity displays. In telling us the story of that memorable evening, Luke devotes twenty-four verses, and John occupies five whole chapters, but Mark concentrates all into nine brief verses (17-25); he fastens upon the two outstanding facts: the announcement of the betrayal and the institution of the supper. It would seem, from John's narrative, that between these Judas went out, so that he was not at what we call the Lord's Supper. Perhaps the announcement of the betrayal was designed to get rid of Judas before this supper was instituted.

When something goes wrong we should always think of ourselves before we suspect anyone else: *'Is it I?'* In this inquiry is evidence of both fear and hope: fear of oneself, and hope of the other disciples. One in that circle of twelve was a traitor; let us hope that the proportion is not as great today.

The supper is the Lord's *forget-me-not*; and unspeakably sad it is that that which was designed to unite all his people, has proved more than anything else, to be so divisive. Too often Christ is obscured by the cross, and the symbol takes the place of the Saviour. Such things as *fasting communion, transubstantiation, reservation,* and *sacerdotalism,* have destroyed 'the simplicity which is in Christ Jesus'. The holding of a united communion service in the tent at Keswick in July, 1928, did more, as a display of Christian unity, than talk about church union is likely to do in a generation.

How amazing are verses 27,28! Here are darkness and light, loneliness and fellowship, dread and hope. Christ was conscious of the on-coming night, but he was also sure of the daybreak beyond.

Thought: To be true to Christ is to triumph.

In the garden

In the garden (32-42). Let me say what are the things that impress me as I read this solemn record. The first is **Christ's sorrow** (34). He alone with reason could say, *'Behold, and see if there be any sorrow like unto my sorrow.'* What do you suppose was the *cause* and what the *nature* of this sorrow? Well was he called *'a man of sorrows, and acquainted with grief'!*

Then, **Christ's loneliness** (35). *'He went forward a little.'* First he left the eight, and then the three. All real greatness is lonely, and all deep sorrow is lonely. The highest mountains court the terrible solitudes. Even in a crowd Christ must have been lonely, but scarcely ever so lonely as in the deep shadow of these olive trees. And, let it be said, all who follow him closely will have this experience of loneliness.

The next thing that impresses me is **Christ's yieldedness** (36): *'Not what I will, but what thou wilt.'* Let us not suppose that there were here ever two wills, for Christ's will was always to do the Father's will, but in these words we are taken into the realm of his *motive*. He would not sacrifice himself because it was his will so to do, but because it was his Father's will. What is the motive-spring of all you do?

Further, here we discern **Christ's disappointment** (37-41); *'Couldest thou not watch . . . one hour?'* The RV margin in verse 41 reads, *'Do ye sleep on then, and take your rest?'* – an interrogation, not an exhortation. In this dark hour Jesus craved for sympathy, the sympathy that would watch, but alas, he did not get it.

But even this reveals **Christ's consideration** (38). He made allowance for these men being tired, for 'he knoweth our frame; he remembereth that we are dust.' Think today of his *sorrow*, and *loneliness* and *yieldedness* and *disappointment* and *consideration*.

Thought: To disappoint Christ is to fail.

Mock justice

Let us begin at verse 43, and see what happened.

● **At the gate** (43-50). The three figures that stand clearly before us here are Jesus, Judas and Peter. Judas and Peter both did wrong, but vastly different wrong. Judas' was the wrong of basest treachery; Peter's was the wrong of reckless enthusiasm; the one was the wrong of hate, the other of love; and these wrongs were very differently judged.

What a mystery Judas is! Was he an incarnate demon? (John 6:70). Only twice do we read of Jesus being *kissed*, once by a man, Judas: once by a woman unnamed (Luke 7:38), and in each case the word is 'kissed him much'. As above, how vast the difference between these kisses! Here again, are hate and love. Opposite things may express themselves in the same way. Actions, in themselves, have no moral value; it is the motive which supplies that.

● **On the way** (51,52). There can be little doubt that this *'certain young man'* was Mark himself; and here is a third contrast. Peter's enthusiasm leapt into flame (47), but Mark's died out in smoke. Peter's was fierce to the point of folly, but Mark's was cautious to the point of cowardice. For the business of such a night as that, *a linen cloth* was of no use: *'the whole armour of God'* was needed.

● **Before the Sanhedrin** (53-65). The trial of Jesus was in two parts: one ecclesiastical, the other civil. The ecclesiastical trial was in three stages: (a) before Annas; (b) before the Sanhedrin by night; (c) before the Sanhedrin in the morning. In the ecclesiastical trial the charge was *blasphemy*; in the civil trial, it was *treason*. Humanly speaking, the fate of Jesus was determined at a trial which was illegal (53-65). Remember that he of whom all this is written was the Son of God! And he endured all that *for me!*

Thought: 'Consider him who endured such contradiction of sinners against himself.'

Confession and denial

Two matters claim our attention here: a confession and a denial.

● **The confession** (60-65). Here, *Christ plainly claims to be God* (61,62). Please ponder that, for it either is or is not so, and either way it eternally matters. If this claim be not true, there is no salvation for you and for me; but if it be true, then the whole world is under necessity to relate itself to the fact. '*Art thou the Christ (the fulfilment of the messianic hope), the Son of the Blessed?*' Jesus said, '*I am.*' They said, '*Ye have heard the blasphemy.*'

This is a tremendous passage, and the value of the whole New Testament depends upon it. Did Christ speak blasphemy? Then listen to the roar of nineteen hundred years of Christianity crumbling into chaos. As for me, I stake my welfare for time and eternity upon the truthfulness of what Jesus then said.

● **The denial** (66-72). This is indeed a sad affair. And it is also a solemn warning, for numberless people *are* in danger of doing what Peter did. The next worse thing to betrayal is denial of Christ, and really denial is a form of betrayal. Let no one say that Peter was a coward; he was not. The man who struck out at the garden gate was no coward. The breakdown in the courtyard is that of a strong, not of a weak man.

He made three great mistakes. The first was his *self-confidence*: '*Though all shall be caused to stumble, yet will not I*' (29). Such a faith is the forerunner of a fall. The second mistake was in his *running into the danger zone* (66; John 18:15,16). It was not cowardice, that took him there, but confidence. None of us has any right to court trouble. If you play with fire, don't be surprised if you get burnt. His third mistake was that instead of confessing, he *compromised* (68, RV margin).

Thought: To deny Christ is death.

The crisis of choice

We have said that the ecclesiastical trial of Jesus was in three stages. So also was the civil trial: (a) before Pilate; (b) before Herod; (c) before Pilate again. In verses 1-5 we have the first of these. The high priest had asked Jesus if he were the Son of God, and he said he was (14:61,62); now Pilate asks him if he is the king of the Jews, and he says he is (2). The divine Son, the messianic King: these are his claims; there was nothing more to say, and so, after this, *'Jesus no more answered anything'* (5, RV).

There never is any use in continuing to teach those who are rejecting the light they already have. In no school is x, y, z, taught where a, b, c has not been learned. Christ's silence is a solemn thing, for it is virtually a verdict on his examiners. Poor Pilate! He knew what was right, but failed to do it; he saw the light but did not follow it, and so he is branded for all time, and I fear, for all eternity.

The third and final stage of Jesus' trials was the most protracted of the three (6-15). Mark seizes upon what was vital in it, passing over many details. Tradition says the full name of this man was Jesus Barabba; Bar-abba, meaning 'son of the father', and father meaning 'rabbi'. He was, therefore, a man of good family, who had fallen into ways of crime. The Jews, therefore, sacrifice the *'Son of the Blessed'* (14:61) for a *son of a rabbi*; and with not a semblance of reason, for Barabbas actually was guilty of the crime with which they falsely charged Jesus (7, see John 19:12).

But there never is any consistency in sin. Jesus, or Barabbas? Both stood for a kingdom: the one for a heavenly, the other for an earthly kingdom. One stood for faith in goodness, the other, for faith in the sword; the one for love, and the other for violence; and we know which the Jews chose. Which have you chosen?

Thought: When the heart is wicked the judgement is wrong.

Golgotha

Is there a more dreadful picture in the whole range of narrative than that in verses 16-20? This chapter is best read on one's knees and in solitude. The cruelty of the Roman cohort, some 600 soldiers, is beyond comprehension. Why were not the two malefactors treated like this? Why was Jesus? *Why?* Just because the presence of holiness, and love, and godliness, drew into evidence and stung into action sin and hate, and devilry – heaven opened the mouth of hell and the place just reeked with the stench of the pit.

Behold him! Dressed in a cast-off robe, holding a reed, wearing a crown of thorns, buffetted and battered. It was God they were treating in that way; yes, God! And as though all that he had already endured were not enough, they made him carry his own cross until he dropped beneath it. What an indictment of the human race!

But, thank God, these do not represent all. There were his mother, and Martha, and Mary, and Joseph of Arimathaea, and Nicodemus, and Simon of Cyrene, and others. Is there a Christian in the world who would not give his life to have done for Jesus what Simon did? He became Jesus' substitute, who was so soon to become his (21).

And then, the crucifixion (22-32). It is better to think than to speak here; but let us seize upon one thought: *'He saved others; can he not save himself?'* What a declaration! And what an implication! This was not the first time, nor the last, that Christ's enemies spoke truly of him. The Saviour must be sacrificed, for salvation is only by suffering. And the amazing thing about all this is that *he need not have done it!* It was not the nails that held him to the tree, but his own unquenchable love for you and me. Do you believe that?

Thought: Only my all can satisfy his love.

The Saviour dies

The death of Christ! History tells us of many deaths: deaths tragic, cruel, noble, pathetic; but this one stands alone among them all. Both Christ's entrance into, and exit from, the world were unique, as was the life which was lived between the two. He chose to be born, and he chose to die, and no one else that ever lived did either. Mark's usual brevity characterises his account of what happened (33-39).

We can do here, only that which the women did, *'behold from afar'* (40), for who can penetrate this mystery? It was terrible for Jesus in such an hour to be forsaken by his disciples, but who can tell what it meant to him to be forsaken by his father (34)? How awful must have been that Hebrew cry at three o'clock that afternoon!

That middle cross was the one on which Barabbas would have died. But he had been released. Almost certainly he would be in that crowd, and would look upon him who had taken his place. Was he turned to God in that hour, as Simon of Cyrene had been? Perhaps we shall see Barabbas in heaven.

When the men fled, the women followed Jesus, and, worse than torture though it must have been to them, they watched to see the end (40,41). Blessed women! They had helped him while he lived, and now they stand by him while he dies. There is nothing so unconquerable as the love of a true woman.

Christ had many secret disciples, and some of these avowed their faith in this dread hour, as stars come out when night comes on. Joseph was one of these (42-46). Why did he not stand by and help him while he lived? So many people keep all their flowers for the coffin. Do not do that!

Thought: I will do what I can while I may.

The empty tomb

● **Love** (1-4). These dear and devoted women beheld the crucifixion (15:40), and they were careful to observe where the body of their loved one was laid (15:47). As soon as the Sabbath was ended, they bought spices, and *'very early'* the next morning they were at the tomb. Where were Peter, and James, and John, and the others? Be it to the eternal credit of these women that they loved well enough to take risks and make sacrifices.

Their love *lasted*, yes, right through darkness and death to the resurrection morning, and their love was *lavish*. There was no nice calculation here. Nicodemus had already bestowed a hundred pounds' weight of spices on the body and tomb; but that was his love, not theirs; they must bring their own gift, the best and most they could give.

And their love was *eager*. Overnight they had talked together and arranged when and where they would meet, and they did not 'sleep in' the next morning. By the light of the rising sun, and the bracing morning air they hastened to the tomb, discussing how they were to get the great stone rolled from its mouth, yet determined it should be done. Do we love like that? The last thing at night? The first thing in the morning? And all through the day?

● **Victory** (5-8). What a difference it would have made to us all if more often we had seen *the angel at the grave* (5); radiant life in the place of death! *'He is risen; he is not here.'* The mighty deed is done; the victory is won; death is destroyed and the grave is conquered.

The light of that Easter morning floods all the landscape of gospel story. Then, *'go . . . tell'* (7). Who dare keep such news as this to himself?

Christ is risen! What difference does it make to you? Can you faintly imagine what life would be if he had not risen? The cross, the grave, the throne; that is the way he went, and he calls us to go with him, all the way. Will you?

Thought: Hallelujah! What a Saviour!

The same Jesus

These verses, though not in the two oldest Greek manuscripts, are, nevertheless, a record very ancient and authentic. The dominating notes of the gospel story are – incarnation, preparation, ministration, crucifixion, resurrection, manifestation and ascension. This passage tells us of some of the things that happened during the forty days between Christ's resurrection and ascension. There seem to have been ten appearances – five on the day of the resurrection, and five after. Of these, Mark records three: (a) to Mary Magdalene; (b) to two disciples on the way to Emmaus; (c) to the eleven.

Have you ever observed that only disciples ever saw the Lord in resurrection life? Why did he not go to Pilate, or appear in the midst of the Sanhedrin? And of all his disciples, he appeared first to a woman. Why? Because her love put her in the way of such a blessing. After having left the tomb, with the others, she returned to it, and her devotion was greatly rewarded (9-11). The full story of the second appearance (12,13) we get in Luke 24; and the third in Luke 24:36-43 and John 20:19-25.

The unbelief of the disciples is truly amazing (11,13). No wonder the Lord 'upbraided them' (14). But he did not abandon them. These so ordinary and faithless men are given a supreme opportunity: they are made the custodians of the gospel, and given the world for a sphere.

Nothing in history is more wonderful than the fact that a handful of unschooled men were put in charge of the greatest enterprise of all the ages, and without any material resources or temporal facilities, faced up to impossible odds, and gloriously won through! Account for it? 'The Lord working with them, and confirming the word by the signs that followed' (20, RV). So ends a story than which nothing is greater in human annals, and we see the Lord Jesus on the throne.

Thought: Come, see – go tell.